POLICING
TRANSPORTATION FACILITIES

ABOUT THE AUTHORS

Henry I. DeGeneste

Mr. DeGeneste is the retired Director of Public Safety and Superintendent of Police for the Port Authority of New York and New Jersey Police, where he directed the operations for securing the metropolitan New York/New Jersey airports, bridges, tunnels, trains, seaports and other vital transit infrastructure. He had a long and distinguished career in law enforcement leading to this position. He is the past President of the National Organization of Black Law Enforcement Executives (NOBLE), and former member of the Board of Directors of the Police Executive Research Forum (PERF). He is presently serving as a Commissioner on the National Commission on Accreditation of Law Enforcement Agencies (CALEA), and is currently employed as a Senior Vice President and Director of Corporate Security for Prudential Securities, Inc. He earned a Bachelor of Arts degree in Business Management from Adelphi University. Together with John P. Sullivan, he has authored numerous articles on transit and other law enforcement topics for such journals as *The Police Chief* and *Criminal Justice the Americas.*

John P. Sullivan

Mr. Sullivan is a police officer for a major Southern California police agency who has extensive planning experience in the region's return to rail transit. He is the founding editor of *Transit Policing: A Journal for the Transit Police Service.* He was the former Homeless Coordinator at the Port Authority of New York and New Jersey's Journal Square Transportation Center, and holds a Master of Arts degree in Urban Affairs and Policy Analysis from the New School for Social Research, and a Bachelor of Arts degree in government and international relations from the College of William and Mary. Together with Henry I. DeGeneste, he has authored numerous articles on transit and other law enforcement issues for such journals as *Criminal Justice the Americas* and *The Police Chief,* and has an extensive list of publishing credits under his own name in police and emergency management periodicals such as *Prehospital and Disaster Medicine* and the *American Fire Journal.*

POLICING TRANSPORTATION FACILITIES

By

HENRY I. DeGENESTE

and

JOHN P. SULLIVAN

CHARLES C THOMAS • PUBLISHER
Springfield • Illinois • U.S.A.

Published and Distributed Throughout the World by

CHARLES C THOMAS • PUBLISHER
2600 South First Street
Springfield, Illinois 62794-9265

© *1994 by* CHARLES C THOMAS • PUBLISHER

ISBN 0-398-05929-2

Library of Congress Catalog Card Number: 94-26575

Printed in the United States of America
SC-R-3

Library of Congress Cataloging-in-Publication Data

DeGeneste, Henry I.
    Policing transportation facilities / by Henry I. DeGeneste and
John P. Sullivan.
       p.   cm.
    Includes bibliographical references and index.
    ISBN 0-398-05929-2
    1. Transportation facilities—United States—Security measures.
2. Freight and freightage—United States—Security measures.
3. Police—United States.   4. Local transit crime—United States.
I. Sullivan, John P., 1959–   . II. Title.
HV8291.U6D44   1994
363.2'87—dc20   94-26575
                                          CIP

PREFACE

This publication, *Policing Transportation Facilities,* represents several years of literature searches, field interviews and personal experience of the authors. As part of our research, teaching experience, program development, administration and direct provision of service, we often looked for materials to guide our efforts in this field to no avail. We concluded that no single text was available to describe the many facets involved in providing security specifically at transportation facilities.

Recognizing the need and value of such a text to our profession, we set out to document the emerging discipline of transport policing. In the course of this project we came to understand how little was written about this subject. Thus, *Policing Transportation Facilities* is intended as a starting point. We hope it will provide administrators and police at rail and bus transit systems, airports and seaports with a framework for developing strategies to protect their facilities and patrons from current and future security risks.

People, goods and information flow through transportation hubs, bringing communities and cultures together. Just as these facilities can link the positive aspects of a community to those of another, they also can expose those communities to the risks, threats and actuality of crime.

Henry I. DeGeneste
John P. Sullivan

ACKNOWLEDGMENTS

I would like to thank my wife, Anita Adams Sullivan, for her contribution to this text. Her critical eye, patience and tireless typing of numerous drafts and the manuscript did much to enhance the quality of the final product.

J.S.

I would also like to add my thanks to my Administrative Assistant, Althea Becton, for her generous help in getting letters and sample manuscripts out to publishers; and Edna B. Turner for her help in reviewing the final page proofs.

H.D.

CONTENTS

POLICING
TRANSPORTATION FACILITIES

Chapter 1

MOVING THE MASSES

Transportation facilities are a vital link in the economic and social life of communities. Airports, seaports, bus and rail stations and systems, bridges and tunnels provide the loci for the transfer of cargo, people and information from one area to another. Yet each of these vital hubs—much like the communities they connect—can also become links in a variety of criminal activity.

Drug trafficking, terrorism, cargo theft, smuggling, organized crime and the risk of hazardous cargo release are threats to public safety and order. Transport police must face these specialized problems in addition to the "normal" criminal activity handled by their counterparts in general service police agencies. The distinct environment of transportation facilities and the skills needed to adequately police these facilities has resulted in the formation of specialized units within general service agencies, as well as the formation of special purpose transportation police agencies.

Specialized units and agencies patrol many of the world's airports, marine terminals, commuter rail systems, bridges, tunnels, highways, bus systems, and bus and rail terminals. In carrying out their duties, these transport police address the unique needs of the transportation infrastructure.

The maintenance of order and security in transportation facilities impacts the lives of those who use the facilities and those who live and work in the surrounding communities. Thus, an understanding of the crime and order issues specifically related to transit, and the relationship between crime on the system and crime in the surrounding neighborhoods, is a pressing concern.

Police must understand the dynamics involved in policing their specialized environment, and share this understanding with the police community as a whole. Coordination of operations among specialized and general police agencies at all levels of government is essential to success. In the same line, specialized units focusing on separate segments

3

of the transportation network need to broaden their perspective by gathering information from similar transport facilities.

Protecting people and cargo in transit—regardless of transport mode—requires similar skills and an understanding of similar problems and phenomena. In fact, people and goods often utilize a variety of transit modes throughout a single trip. An integrated approach to security and police services is required at all points along the transport chain, and the approach should be based on communication, coordination and mutual respect. Only through such integration can persons and property safely move from one point to another.

Policing Transportation Facilities is intended to provide a framework for police, government and transportation administrators in their quest to develop meaningful responses to crime, disorder and threats to public safety which occur in a transit setting. Consequently, this text addresses some of society's most pressing dilemmas: terrorism, drug trafficking, hazardous materials incidents and fear of crime.

We will examine the nature and scope of transportation-related crime and the unique requirements of policing various transportation facilities. It is hoped that this review will assist in the development of crime reduction strategies as well as in the identification of policy and operational issues for local government, transportation center operators, transportation carriers and police.

The remaining chapters of this book examine various aspects of our subject. Chapter 2 reviews the nature and extent of rail and subway crime, while Chapter 3 examines maritime issues. Seaport security, cargo theft and pilferage, along with issues facing vessel masters at port and underway regarding threats to shipboard security, are explored. The need for an integrated approach to these issues will be examined in depth.

Chapter 4 covers the nature and extent of airport crime and aviation security.

Transportation terrorism is the subject of Chapter 5, which deals with the issue as it impacts marine, aviation and rail sites. Information is provided as a basis for developing technological and tactical responses. Essential elements of a comprehensive threat management program are also discussed.

Chapter 6 examines drug trafficking and its impact on the transportation industry, concentrating on the way illegal drugs are channeled through transportation centers. Interdiction and enforcement strategies are discussed.

Hazardous cargo in transit is the focus of Chapter 7, which explores the public safety issues resulting from accidents involving hazardous materials. Bus and rail terminal crime is covered in Chapter 8.

Chapter 9 focuses on the special issues surrounding the homeless and emotionally disturbed populations which congregate in mainly urban transit centers. Finally, Chapter 10 explores the overall role of specialized transport policing. A discussion of common factors found throughout the transportation setting will form the basis for examining the role of transportation centers and police within their communities at large. The interdependent nature of transit crime and general crime will be discussed.

As crime and disorder become critical issues throughout the industrialized world, their impact on the transportation infrastructure can be expected to become key policy concerns. This text is intended to facilitate a meaningful understanding of these issues, and hopefully will serve as a catalyst for professional development among the police responsible for securing these vital facilities.

Chapter 2

COMMUTER RAIL AND SUBWAY CRIME

Passenger rail transportation plays an important role in the cultural and economic life of cities. Each day mass transit systems throughout the world bring workers into cities to staff the range of economic activities necessary for their existence. Traditionally, passenger rail lines have helped to determine the nature of cities by influencing patterns of land use and commercial activity. These rail lines have come in the form of subways, providing transport within the conurbation, and commuter lines, serving to bring people in from surrounding areas. Street or trolley cars help to supplement both forms of rail transit.

With the growing popularity of passenger automobiles, the dominance of rail transit declined. Choked urban freeways and pollution, however, have made rail transit a viable transportation alternative once again. Subways are found in major cities around the world: New York, London, Buenos Aires, Paris, Moscow, Hong Kong, among others. Commuter rail lines are also planned and several cities—Los Angeles, San Diego, Portland and Buffalo, for example—have developed trolley or light-rail lines.

The largest systems are in New York (the New York City subway, the PATH system, the Staten Island Rapid Transit and the Newark City subway), 263 miles long moving over 1.1 billion passengers yearly; London, 260 miles and 655 million passengers; Paris, 157 miles and 1.25 billion passengers; and Tokyo, with 122 miles and 1.5 billion passengers. The use of mass rail transportation is on the rise worldwide, particularly considering the rapid urbanization of the third world.

The Police Role

The prominence of rail transit and the large numbers of people who utilize it make the safety and security of transit systems an important concern. Subway and commuter rail crime obviously varies in extent, severity and type from city to city and within cities themselves, yet crime is a concern of all operators of transit systems. To cope with this problem and to assure the safe operation of their systems, many rail transit authorities maintain police forces. Others rely on municipal police agencies to patrol the systems. In either case, the mission of police in a transit environment remains the same—to prevent crime, arrest offenders, maintain passenger and employee safety and generally secure the rapid transit system. "Given the financial pressures on public transit operations and a strong national interest in promoting greater use of mass transit, it becomes important to examine the effectiveness of various transit policing methods in controlling crime and alleviating the public's fear of insecurity."[1]

The London Underground and the Paris Metropolitan subways are policed by centralized national transit police forces. The Chicago Loop transit system is policed by the Chicago Police Department. The Washington, D.C., Metro is policed by a tri-state (Washington, D.C., Maryland, Virginia) metro police force, and the New York-New Jersey PATH interstate commuter rail system is policed by the bi-state multiple special function Port Authority Police.

One of the largest transportation police agencies in the world is the New York City Transit Police Department. The New York City Transit Police patrol the world's largest mass transit system, the New York City subway. Providing transport to over 3.4 million riders daily in a system with 465 stations, the New York City subway operates over 6,200 rail passenger cars—or more cars than all other rapid transit lines in the United States combined, including regional commuter rail systems and Amtrak, the national rail passenger system.

The New York City Transit Police Department is among the twelve largest police agencies in the U.S., and is larger than the municipal departments of Boston, San Francisco and Kansas City. The department originated in 1933 as the six-member New York City Independent Subway Special Police. It had expenditures of $162.7 million in 1984[2] and was 4,200 members strong by 1992.[3] By fiscal year 1990 (July 1989–June 1990) total expenditures were approximately $277 million according to the New York City Transit Police Department September 1990 Monthly Management Report.

The transit environment entails markedly different challenges to transit police and requires the adoption of police strategies which are tailored to address the special needs of this environment. While not a separate discipline from policing in general, there are many unique aspects which require special training or familiarization for the achievement of effective policing.

Transit Crime

The physical surroundings, higher levels of noise, and isolation from the surface and normal fixtures of urban life on the street often leave riders feeling fearful, confined and claustrophobic. Passenger perceptions such as these make a police officer's job more difficult, since he or she must manage people who view themselves as being in a strange environment and who, as such, may not react in the same way while riding the subway as they would when off the system. Considering these environmental difficulties, how much crime actually exists on the subways? What types of crime are encountered?

E.J. Thrasher and J.R. Schnell, in "Scope of Crime and Vandalism on Urban Transit Systems,"[4] suggest that a person is twice as likely to be involved in crime in a transit situation as he or she is in a nontransit situation, while in Philadelphia it was found that the risk on the subway was equal to that of the street.[5] In 1985, 97 percent of crime in New York City occurred above ground in the street and only 3 percent occurred in the subway.[6] The following table of felony crimes reported on the New York City subway for the years 1979–1992 demonstrates some of the problems faced by transit police.

Different levels of transit crime exist within cities, and from city to city. The exact extent of the problem thus must be considered variable and inconclusive. Beyond quantity of incidents, more is known about the quality of transit crime. In a study of fifteen U.S. and Canadian transit systems,[7] Larry G. Richards and Lester A. Hoel reported the following major problems. Robbery, larceny and serious assault accounted for most incidents against persons, while serious vandalism, public inebriation and disorderly conduct constituted the most frequently encountered crime against property. While such acts as public inebriation and disorderly conduct did not immediately endanger the public, such activities contributed to decreased passenger perceptions of safety.

In 1983, for example, the New York City Transit Authority reported 13,596 felonies, an 11.5 percent drop from 1982 (with 15,364 felonies). In 1983 there were 576,631 felonies in all of New York City. Transit Police expenditures for 1983 were $142.2 million, and 1982 expenditures totaled $130.6 million.[8] In the first half of 1985, the Transit Police Department

Table 1-1. Total Felony Crime Reported on New York City Subway, 1979–1992.

	1979	1980	1981	1982	1983
Total Felonies	10,897	12,907	15,295	15,368	13,596
Homicides	16	20	14	17	5
Rapes or attempts	32	24	36	34	40
Robberies	4,014	5,009	6,628	6,778	5,612
Felonies assault	643	562	756	903	838
Burglaries	195	238	316	291	250
Grand larcenies	5,522	6,416	6,553	6,283	6,009
Other felonies	475	638	992	1,062	842

	1984	1985	1986	1987	1988
Total Felonies	14,000	12,841	14,030	13,000	14,306
Homicides	9	11	11	7	12
Rapes or attempts	21	28	27	25	34
Robberies	5,998	5,414	5,688	5,390	6,529
Felonies assault	901	897	981	991	1,203
Burglaries	225	157	182	207	240
Grand larcenies	5,996	5,583	6,498	5,694	5,703
Other felonies	850	751	643	686	585

	1989	1990	1991	1992	
Total Felonies	16,906	18,324	15,572	133,250	
Homicides	20	26	25*	20	
Rapes or attempts	27	33	31	22	
Robberies	8,267	9,297	8,203	6,221	
Felonies assault	1,184	1,353	1,115	967	
Burglaries	279	174	129	167	
Grand larcenies	6,486	6,614	5,102	4,802	
Other felonies	643	827	967	1,051	

*Includes 5 deaths classified as homicide that
resulted from train derailment at 14th Street.
Source: New York City Transit Police Department, Office of Media Services

made 13,687 arrests, issued 187,317 summonses, made 9,696 youth division referrals, ejected 6,248 persons for minor violations and removed 1,737 homeless individuals for referral to municipal shelters.[9] Forcible robbery, followed by grand larceny, are the most frequently reported felonies on the New York City subway. Fare evasion, vandalism, graffiti and petty theft are among the minor crimes committed by juveniles. A Rand Corporation study reported that the average subway robber in New York City is a young black male, 17 years of age, who is usually unarmed.[10] Often groups of young men on their way home from school in the afternoon commit these minor crimes. In contrast, the average token booth robber as noted in the Rand study is 22 years old, usually armed, and operates alone or with a single partner.[11] When token booths were "hardened" with the installation of bullet-resistant glass, some robbers began to use the injection of flammable aerosols or gasoline as weapons, threatening to ignite the substance if not given money or tokens.

The National Institute of Law Enforcement and Criminal Justice in its report *Policing Urban Mass Transit Systems* found that transit crime was largely a problem of the nation's larger cities and that transit crime patterns generally reflected the patterns found in the surrounding areas. Increases in transit crime paralleled increases in street crime. The perpetrators of transit crime and their victims also closely resembled their street counterparts.[12]

Then why are transit systems perceived as being unduly crime-ridden? Subway cars, platforms and passageways are enclosed areas which restrict movement and limit avenues of escape. Many older urban transit systems are plagued by a stigma of neglect. "If the station is dirty, smelly, noisy and filled with graffiti, then users will view it as less secure because these cues are generally associated with unsafe environments."[13] This sensory aggravation also can lead to hostility which may exacerbate the crime-prone nature of the surrounding neighborhoods. "Perceived security, not actual security, is what influences ridership and transit use patterns."[14] As we will see, perceptions of security also influence transit crime. Keeping this in mind, transit operators and police need to maximize both actual and perceived security levels on the transit system.

The perception of security may also contribute to the fact that most transit crime occurs in stations rather than on trains, since the presence of train crews probably reduces or displaces on-train crime. Location, however, cannot be discounted. "An analysis of the activity patterns of subway robbers showed that collectively they concentrate on a small number of stations and portions of train routes, but otherwise there were no common characteristics that would provide guidance for police deployment. The stations and portions of routes having the highest robbery rates tend to lie underneath those parts of the city where robbery rates are also high."[15] This knowledge gives clues to the police administrator for the handling of transit crime. Efforts should be concentrated in those areas where it is perceived that crime will occur. By using a variety of strategies, perception can be modified. These strategies will be discussed later in this chapter, but immediate consideration should be given to the need for coordination and cooperation with adjacent general service police agencies. Since many transit police operations will be focused within the bounds of areas which correspond with off-system high crime districts, cooperation and coordination are especially important. The same is true for commuter rail systems.

Transit police and security measures are generally accepted as elements of successful urban mass transit systems. The factors that make transit policing an integral element of successful urban systems are equally important in a suburban commuter or regional rail setting. While problems of crime and disorder are generally less severe on regional commuter systems, they still exist.

Regional commuter rail systems throughout the world share common problems. Key concerns include quality-of-life issues such as disorderly passengers, vandalism and graffiti. Additional concerns are fare evasion and fare disputes, trespassing, obstructions placed on tracks, train stonings, auto theft and vehicle burglaries at park-and-ride areas, and tampering with critical signal devices (including metal thefts). Also encountered are counterfeit fare media, employee theft and fraud, and to a lesser degree, passenger robberies and purse snatchings.

Additional public safety concerns shared by commuter rail systems are critical incidents such as fires, grade crossing accidents, natural disasters, train collisions and derailments and bomb threats.

Regional rail services move relatively large numbers of people in a compressed space. This dynamic requires that railways provide a mechanism for ensuring passenger assistance, crowd management and response to on-system emergencies. Smooth and effective management of unplanned events allows the railway to operate at peak efficiency, minimizing delays and service disruptions.

The bulk of criminal activity on commuter rail lines consists of vandalism by juveniles or crimes committed in the system's terminals, which are often in inner city areas (transportation terminals and their problems will be addressed in Chapter 8).

Both juveniles and the habitues of terminals who are involved in criminal activity on-system are also likely to participate in similar off-system activity. Coordinating efforts and sharing information will result in more efficient utilization of police service by both agencies and will help to increase the effectiveness of crime abatement activities both on and off the system.

Graffiti

Graffiti and vandalism are problems which have plagued transit systems in recent years. Both tend to convey negative security perceptions to riders. In addition to careful design efforts which consider the input of behavioral psychologists and environmental engineers to determine the desirable level of lighting and physical layout, the system should be cleaned and painted frequently. Preventive maintenance combined with active police enforcement of minor crimes and offenses which erode perceptions of safety can discourage deviant activity and encourage legitimate primary system usage.

The reduction of vandalism and graffiti is believed to support positive user perceptions, which lead to increased ridership and reductions in crime. Many systems have found that the quick removal of graffiti helps to discourage continued graffiti assaults. Among the systems which have reported this trend are PATH, the Newark City Subway, and the New York City Transit Authority.

In an effort to curb the scourge of graffiti in New York City, the Transit Authority developed a graffiti control program. The program is a joint effort of the Transit Authority's Car Equipment Department's Car Appearance Unit and the New York City Transit Police. Coordinated through the Car Appearance Unit, the program is based on the premise that removing graffiti reduces the incentive to create new graffiti. By September 1985, one-third of the Transit Authority fleet was enrolled in the graffiti-free program. By 1989, the program succeeded in keeping all its rail cars virtually graffiti-free.

The program has several components: the removal of new graffiti within 24 hours of its appearance; the deployment of uniformed and plainclothes Transit Police on graffiti-free trains and in other identified trouble spots such as lay-ups or holding areas; and improved security (such as fencing, lighting and alarms) and surveillance at Transit Authority yards and lay-ups.

While it is difficult if not impossible to statistically analyze which component of the graffiti-free program has had the greatest impact, most Transit Authority administrators feel that the program has been overwhelmingly successful by depriving graffiti "artists" of their public message board (see Table 1-2).

Since its inception, the New York City Transit Authority's Clean Car Program has become an industry-wide model. Similar approaches have

Table 1-2. Clean Car Program (NYCTA) Goals and Achievements, 1984–1989.

Year	Clean Cars	
	Goal	Actual
1984	—	400
1985	1720	1915
1986	3434	3454
1987	4707	4839
1988	5946	6077
1989	6221	6245

Source: NYCTA Clean Car Program

been credited with keeping new light rail systems—such as the San Diego Trolley and Los Angeles' Metro Blue Line—virtually graffiti-free. For an excellent discussion of the Clean Car Program, particularly its underlying management commitment, problem-oriented basis and interdisciplinary approach, see "Subway Graffiti in New York City: 'Gettin' Up' vs. 'Meaning It and Cleanin' It'" by Maryalice Sloan-Howitt and George L. Kelling in *Security Journal,* 1990 Vol. 1, No. 3.

Fare Evasion

Fare evasion is another problem which concerns all rail transit systems. Transit systems rely upon fare revenue to recover varying proportions of their operating revenue. When riders utilize the system without paying the proper fare, this "farebox recovery" ratio is reduced, placing a fiscal burden upon the system.

Fare collection is achieved through a variety of methods. Subways and urban railways traditionally relied upon the turnstile to provide a barrier through which patrons must pass, after depositing their fare, to gain entry to the system. Farebeats overcame this barrier by slipping in between the prongs of the turnstile or jumping over it altogether. Alternatively, farebeats would enter through service or exit gates.

Higher gates, electronically triggered service gates, closed circuit television surveillance and the positioning of police officers, security guards or civilian monitors at the turnstile area have been applied as countermeasures. Plainclothes surveillance has also been used to detect and apprehend fare violators on systems using turnstile entry.

While plainclothes surveillance and uniformed patrol of fare zones can result in lowered fare evasion rates, these measures are labor intensive and thus costly. This type of deployment can also be tedious and boring duty, leading to a morale problem among highly motivated police personnel.

Advances in technology have brought other types of automated fare collection. The magnetic fare card allows systems to reduce the use of slugs or counterfeit tokens in turnstiles. It often requires the patron to use the card for exit as well as entrance to the system, thus allowing a flexible fare structure based on zones. These systems can still be circumvented, however, and require labor intensive efforts to limit fare evasion.

Regional commuter railways have traditionally relied upon on-board fare collection by train crews or conductors. The on-board presence of a conductor minimizes fare evasion but the conductor must handle cash, increasing the opportunity for employee fraud and making the conductor a potential target of robbery. The conductor is also exposed to conflict as the result of confronting violators. These conflicts, known as fare disputes, frequently necessitate a police response.

Many of North America's newer light rail systems have adopted the European practice of barrier-free, proof-of-payment fare collection. Under this type of system, fare compliance is gained through periodic fare checks by uniformed fare compliance personnel. Fare compliance personnel may be either sworn police officers, as in Los Angeles and Baltimore; security officers, as on South Florida's Tri-Rail system; or uniformed fare inspectors with limited fare enforcement authority, as in San Diego, Sacramento, Buffalo and numerous Canadian systems.

Regardless of the status of fare inspectors, patrons utilizing a barrier-free system are required to purchase valid proof-of-payment prior to entering a designated fare paid zone. Fare paid zones may be narrowly designated as on-board railcars or more broadly defined to include station platforms and waiting areas. The broader definition gives police more flexibility in regulating patron behavior and disorder.

Typically, patrons purchase their fare from a self-service ticket vending machine located outside the fare zone. At the entrance to the fare paid zone, signs are posted advising patrons of the fare structure and the requirement to have a valid form of fare payment in their possession at all times within the system.

Compliance with fare policy is ensured through periodic, unannounced checks by roving fare inspectors. The success of a barrier-free proof-of-payment system is dependent upon regular fare checks throughout the system. Inspectors must avoid fixed patterns of inspection. Experience on the majority of systems utilizing this format demonstrates that approximately 25 percent of the system's ridership needs to be checked to ensure an acceptable rate of compliance. The barrier-free format has been successful on light rail systems, with systems in San Diego and Los Angeles, for example, consistently achieving evasion rates of less than one percent.

Two statistics are important to calculating the success of a barrier-free fare compliance format: the inspection rate and the evasion rate. In order to calculate the inspection rate, the number of patrons or passengers (PAX) inspected is divided by the total ridership, then multiplied by one hundred.

Formula for calculating inspection rate

$$\frac{\text{\# PAX Inspected} \times 100}{\text{Total PAX}} = \text{Inspection Rate}$$

The degree of fare evasion detected by inspectors among those passengers inspected (i.e., the evasion rate of a sample of total riders) is the evasion rate. It is calculated by dividing the number of evaders detected by the number of passengers inspected, then multiplying by one hundred.

Formula for calculating evasion rate

$$\frac{\text{\# Evaders Detected} \times}{\text{\# PAX Inspected}} 100 = \text{Evasion Rate}$$

Accurate inspection and evasion rates are dependent upon the generation of accurate inspection activity logs. When designing an inspection program, efforts must be taken to minimize nonrandom patterns of inspection which may skew the sample statistics.

Both sworn police officers and nonsworn code enforcement personnel are used to perform fare enforcement duties. While selection of the class of personnel for fare inspection and enforcement is a system-specific issue, dependent upon local laws, practice and individual system conditions, advantages of both models can be summarized. Among the advantages of nonsworn personnel are:

- Inspectors can be deployed separate from crime and disorder control concerns, allowing the flexibility to maintain control of

the number of inspections in a closer to random manner which approximates ridership patterns.
- Nonsworn inspectors in many cases can be hired at a lower cost and can be subject to greater flexibility in shift deployment.
- Costs of training and insurance are often lower.

Drawbacks to nonsworn inspectors include the need to summon police to handle more complex incidents, and the need for police to transport violators for booking and processing subsequent to arrest — a duplication of service.

Advantages of using sworn inspectors include:

- Enhanced patron perceptions of security due to heightened police visibility.
- The ability of police to employ a wider range of discretionary judgment to resolve disputes, since police officers have a wider range of possible actions at their disposal.
- Sworn officers can develop ongoing relationships with system users, enhancing the ability to gather criminal intelligence and enhancing familiarity with the system and its needs.
- Supervisory, support and clerical functions are streamlined, limiting the duplication of supporting services.

Drawbacks of using police to perform inspection duties include the perception among police officers that this is not a true police function, with the resulting drop in officer morale.

Regardless of the type of personnel conducting fare compliance duties, fare compliance is a vital function which needs to be integrated into a system's total security package. The vigorous enforcement of fare and quality-of-life violations can contribute to enhanced patron perceptions of security, and minimize actual disorder on the system.

Transit Strategies

Several strategies can be used for overall security of transit systems, including:

- police operations, including uniformed and plainclothes patrol;
- closed circuit television monitoring (CCTV) and/or passenger alert devices;

- manipulation of environmental design factors, including increased lighting and target "hardening";
- limiting operations, including off-hour closure of stations, shorter trains, consolidation of passenger use areas.

Most transit systems have found that a combination of the above strategies, tailored in accordance with local exigencies, is the most effective way to combat transit crime. Since passenger perceptions of transit crime and security influence both ridership patterns and actual crime itself, the strategies chosen must affect passenger perceptions in a positive manner.

Perceptions of security are the greatest tools in combatting crime. Manipulation of perceptions is a useful countermeasure since improved perceptions increase ridership. When ridership goes up, with the resulting higher number of people using the system, opportunities for many types of crime are reduced since the isolated situations which foster victimization are limited. Higher concentrations of people, however, may also increase the opportunity for crimes such as pickpocketing or jewelry and purse snatching. Perhaps the most effective means of improving passenger perceptions is the obvious presence of uniformed police and civilian transit staff. Of the two, police presence is vital.

Police can be deployed in a transit environment in a variety of ways. Among the most common methods of deployment currently in use are:

- fixed posts, with an officer assigned to one station or area;
- riding patrol, with officers riding trains on their route;
- mobile/random patrol, with one officer covering several stations on random basis;
- saturation patrol, with large numbers of police officers stationed in specific locations to maximize visibility;
- decoy operations, where officers pose as potential victims;
- stakeouts, concentrating on covert surveillance of an area such as token booths, turnstile areas or a revenue shipment;
- canine patrol, utilizing police-dog teams.

Patrols can be on a uniformed or plainclothes basis. Most transit police agencies rely on a mix of fixed, riding and random patrols.

In 1974, the Rand Corporation reported the results of a retrospective study of policing on the New York City subway system. This study evaluated the effectiveness of an increase in the level of uniformed patrol on the New York City subway. Rand found that the increase of the

Transit Police Department from 1,219 to 3,100 officers in 1965, coupled with intensive saturation patrol of the transit system (officers patrolled every train and station between 20:00 and 04:00), resulted in a genuine and substantial decrease in crime. From this, Rand interpolated that saturated uniformed patrol on the subway had a deterrent effect, at a cost of $35,000 per felony crime deterred (in 1975 dollars). In the short run, no displacement occurred but later it was noted that crime was displaced to daytime hours when there were a lower number of officers present and a decreased intensity of patrol.

To cope with the possibility of displacement, Rand concluded that flexible deployment of patrol resources should be implemented in order to permit more personnel to be focused on high crime times and locations. It is possible, however, that the concentration of police resources in one specific area (such as saturation patrol) may also result in displacement of criminal activity. Therefore, cooperation and coordination both within the transit system and with external police agencies is crucial. Close monitoring of the effects of patrol, personnel and tactical deployment is also important. The following example demonstrates this need.

In 1973 the Philadelphia Police Department, using a $1 million grant, expanded the Philadelphia transit unit from 165 to 195 plainclothes officers and from 20 to 50 canine teams. The anticipated effect of this deployment was a reduction in crimes against both property and persons, and increased clearance rates. It was also hoped that passenger perceptions of security would improve. Surprisingly, such crimes as robbery and assault increased by 1.5 percent while crimes against property, such as vandalism, increased 154 percent. The increased plainclothes presence made it possible to effect more arrests due to increased police availability. As this shows, arrests alone cannot be the sole indicator of the effectiveness of police service delivery.

Police enforcement must be carefully coordinated, providing the proper mix of uniformed and plainclothes personnel. Additionally, consideration must be given to the use of specialized units such as canine teams, helicopter and tactical units. Helicopter units can be used to patrol above ground segments of subways, commuter rail systems, yards and lay-ups.

Public Perceptions

Measures for the effectiveness of police service delivery should include passenger perceptions of crime and security, as well as the more traditional indicators of arrests and clearance rates. Whatever strategy is chosen, intervention should be visible yet subtle. Overfortification should be avoided since it may signal the existence of a crime problem to passengers, decreasing rider perceptions of security.

The National Institute of Law Enforcement and Criminal Justice found that the police strategies which have the greatest positive effect on passenger perceptions are increased police patrol and the installation of passenger alert devices (so that passengers are assured of rapid police response in situations of need). Such alert devices should be simple to operate, well-marked, and hardened to deter vandalism. In-house telephones (station phones) are also useful in this regard — if they are working — since they allow passengers to alert police to situations requiring intervention. These telephones are prone to vandalism, however. Public telephones are also found on many station platforms, but their utility is limited. Many public phones require coins to effect operation and even those phones which allow free emergency calls often link the passenger with local police rather than the transit department. While the call is being transferred to the proper police agency, response time is lengthened. An option to explore may be a transit-specific "911" system for on-system use only. This type of telephone system is currently in use in many airports, where it has proven effective. Also, as telephone technology becomes more deregulated, the cost for this program may be reduced.

Closed circuit television is another option to be considered. Many systems rely on CCTV to supplement security operations. Notable among these are Stockholm's T–Line and the interstate PATH commuter rail line in New York and New Jersey. CCTV can be expensive, however, depending upon the extent of its application. In many older transit stations, CCTV effectiveness is limited because of architectural factors such as the presence of pillars and recesses in walls and corners, which limit the field of observation. Effectiveness may also be reduced by viewer fatigue. On the positive side, CCTV generally enhances the overall perception of safety, and security costs are lower since civilians can monitor viewers, freeing police for patrol. CCTV also appears to have reduced the incidence of graffiti on many transit systems.

Although many systems have found CCTV to be a useful countermeasure for improving security, a New York City Transit Authority experiment at the Columbus Circle subway station in New York discovered an increase in crime. In May 1981, 76 monitors to be viewed by police were put into operation at the station, one of the system's busiest. One year later, in May 1982, "a total of 189 felonies were reported at the station, a 30 percent increase over the previous year."[16]

While the Columbus Circle experiment questions the effectiveness of CCTV as a security countermeasure, it does not mean that CCTV cannot be an effective tool. The utility of CCTV at the Columbus Circle station appeared to be hampered by problems of implementation, since many monitors were poorly wired and installed, and there was an overreliance on the system. It must be remembered that CCTV is meant to be an adjunct to patrol operations and cannot be viewed as a replacement for such action. Additionally, although it has limitations, CCTV positively impacts passenger perceptions. When used as part of a total security package, it can yield positive benefits. For example, modern versions of CCTV have been found effective on newer systems such as Los Angeles' Metro Blue Line light rail, where monitors cover ticket vending machines and platforms on all stations. Police working in a system with well-designed CCTV systems can use them to their advantage, by positioning contacts with violators in the view of a CCTV monitor. Should an incident become complicated, police can request CCTV personnel to tape the incident for future review and potential evidentiary purposes. Also, newer color monitors appear to function better in this application since details are more discernible.

Limiting transit operations is another strategy for improving security. Running shorter trains, closing low-usage stations in high crime areas during off-hours, and consolidating riders to one rather than many platforms can have positive results. When police resources are directed to a smaller, easier to secure area, crime on the system is reduced. A concentration of people also improves perceptions since many people feel there is safety in numbers. There may be public relations drawbacks to this strategy, however, since it may signal a failure to cope with crime by other means, placing the police in a defensive posture. In addition, off-hours riders are given a lower level of service, and these riders are particularly hard hit by such reductions. Frequently these passengers are poor and rely solely on mass transit, having few alternate means of travel.

Improved lighting, spatial arrangement and passenger flow patterns that allow for observation of activities seem safer to passengers, thus addressing transit crime through the improvement of patron perceptions. Since transit systems are often closed in, users feel deprived of control.

Transit system operators can help to alleviate these feelings by adopting the concept of defensible space—the arrangement of space in a manner which fosters a sense of control through the arrangement of physical and psychological barriers.

When designing new stations or rehabilitating older ones, system operators can limit negative, claustrophobic impressions by the use of bright colors, adequate lighting, wide corridors which provide a broad vista of the area to be traversed, and the regulation of passenger flow to keep riders close to "safe zones" such as token booths, passenger assistance phones, newsstands or snack bars, or in sightline of CCTV monitors. Designers should be careful to avoid recesses and potential hiding places, and make it possible for low-use areas to be closed without hampering normal service. Center platforms are preferable to side platforms. Wide windows on cars are better than narrow ones.

Canine Patrol

Another strategy which many transit systems are adopting is canine patrol. Known variously as "K-9," dog-man patrol, etc., canine patrol has benefitted many transit police agencies in its effect on officer morale and improved perceptions of crime on behalf of passengers. No study, however, has demonstrated in a statistically valid way a quantitative decrease in crime resulting from canine deployment.

Canine patrol originated in Europe where police dogs have been used extensively for many years in both Germany and the United Kingdom. One of the earliest police canine training programs was at the Munchen-Freimann Railway Police School in the German Federal Republic.

British police use dogs on an at-need basis to patrol a whole range of transportation and transportation-related facilities including docks, warehouse areas, high value commercial districts, transportation terminals and railways. Additionally, many U.S. transit police agencies have found canine patrol beneficial since the use of canine teams appears to result in a more efficient use of police personnel resources. Using dogs helps to reduce the risk of injury and death to their human partners. With his increased sensory awareness, the dog often provides timely warning of risks, eliminating the element of surprise. "By giving quick warning, the dog often places the officer in the position of having the initiative, an advantage he might otherwise not have."[17]

In addition to routine patrol functions, canine teams are helpful in the tracking of suspects or missing persons, in locating lost or abandoned articles, and in searching buildings and other areas. Dogs can also be helpful in effecting an arrest or preventing the escape of persons who are reasonably believed to have committed a felony. If properly trained, dogs can handle many crowd situations. "Dog and handler support one another and have all the advantages inherent in teamwork."[18]

When embarking on a canine patrol program for a transit environment, the transit police executive must insure the development of guidelines and protocols which fully stipulate canine use and deployment. Also, adequate financial and program support must be assured. Both the dogs and the handlers must be carefully selected and trained.

The canine unit must be smoothly integrated into the existing patrol strategy. This can be aided by familiarizing the entire force and all civilian transit staff with the operations capability of the canine teams, including their limitations. Kenneling, nutrition and veterinary needs must be met.

Training is essential. The initial training for canine teams usually follows a 14-week standard. The Washington, D.C., Metropolitan Police, the New York City Transit Police Department, the London Metropolitan Police and the Port Authority of New York and New Jersey Port Authority Police are among the agencies which follow this 14-week standard. Canine training should include basic animal care, obedience, patrol, building search procedures, tracking, and crowd control.

Potential handlers should be screened for physical fitness, psychological adaptability, and the suitability of their home, home environment and family setting for the inclusion of the dog (since in most cases the dog will live with his officer/handler). Periodic in-service training helps to maintain the dog's proficiency as a police adjunct, and obedience and exercise should be part of the team's daily regimen.

Strategy Effectiveness

While each of the strategies mentioned above can result in a reduction of transit crime, system managers and police administrators have to ask themselves what level of protection they can afford. For the cost, how well will the options work? Will crime be decreased and will passenger perceptions improve? Only careful cost-benefit analysis and program evaluation can provide managers with the informed data needed to make policing strategy decisions.

There are several methods to determine any given strategy's effectiveness. One of the most useful—and the method used by most analysts—is to match the strategy against several criteria such as cost, effectiveness and ease of implementation. Additionally, analysts can generate individual criteria which may be helpful in judging the effectiveness of transit policing strategies.

Criteria for Judging Strategy Effectiveness

1. Station/system factors
   a) design factors
   b) types of crime experienced
   c) rates of crime
2. Funding/staffing factors
3. Community/user factors
   a) community/user acceptance
   b) passenger convenience
4. Security factors
   a) actual security
   b) perceived security
5. Externalities

For each of these factors the analyst, transit operator and police administrator need to measure the projected impact of each of the strategies they may potentially adopt. For example, how will "strategy A" influence station design factors? Will it hamper patron accessibility or will it make the system appear overly defended? Will it alter the types of crime committed? Will it result in reduced crime rates? Are there adequate funds and staff for implementing this strategy, particularly in relation to expected decreases in criminal activity, or will the option be expensive to implement with little measurable effect? Will the system's users accept this new level of intervention or will they feel they are inconvenienced without a measurable return?

Will actual or perceived security be improved? Will one improve at the other's expense or will both decline? Simply stated, externalities are the effect of our actions outside or external to our frame of reference. In the case of a transit policing strategy, what will be the external effects of meeting the goal of crime reduction in a particular area? If a high crime station or transit line is saturated with various crime abatement tools, will crime be displaced to other lines or stations, or off the system to other areas? If so, how much will be displaced and how will transit police deal with this displacement?

Determining the effectiveness of a given strategy through the use of criteria is only part of the work necessary to adopt a course of action for policing transit facilities. Prior to the selection of a strategy, planning is essential. The first stage of planning is *situation assessment,* which considers such questions as: Where are crimes happening? Which types of crime are prevalent? What are the concerns of passengers, system employees and the police who secure the system? Then comes the *definition of the problem* and the *identification of achievable operational goals.* Passenger robbery might be the system's major problem, for example, and achievable operational goals in this case might include the assurance of good communication between passengers and the police, the assurance of rapid police intervention and response, and the enhancement of passengers' perceptions of security. From there, *potential strategies must be defined and evaluated.* This would include defining the types of strategies available, considering various mixes of strategies, and assessing the strategies chosen in light of the criteria generated for determining their effectiveness.

When this process is completed, the optimal strategy must be selected and implemented. *Strategy selection and implementation* will be followed by ongoing *program evaluation.* Since transit crime, like all other crime, is dynamic and always changing, program evaluation alone allows field testing of the selected strategies for their effectiveness. Ongoing evaluation helps to identify externalities and allows the finetuning of strategies to ensure maximal positive effect. Ongoing program evaluation also offers realistic indicators of success and provides a means of guaranteeing flexible strategy deployment.

As mentioned earlier, one of the best measurements of effectiveness of any crime abatement strategy is public perception of security. In an effort to measure the effectiveness of various strategies in this light, J.D. Jacobson, L.G. Richards, C.T. Lerner, L.A. Hoel and A. Branden in the *AGT System Passenger Security Guidebook* convened an experimental panel of six men and four women. The panel ranked a variety of crime abatement strategies as being either "somewhat effective," "very effective" or "having no effect." The findings were used to identify strategies that the riding public would feel were useful. Eighteen crimes were considered: assault, battery, fare evasion, homicide, robbery, purse-snatching, pickpocketing, burglary, vandalism, petty theft, trespassing, arson, missilings, drug violations, sex crimes, drunkenness, disorderly conduct and concealed weapons. The crimes were matched against various strategies in a tabular matrix. From this matrix presented by Richards and Hoel,[19] the following table was constructed. This table shows the relative effectiveness of selected strategies in terms of passenger perception. Strategies rated as "very effective" were given the value of 1; strategies rated "somewhat effective" the value .5. The optimal score was 18.

Table 1-3. Effectiveness of Crime Abatement Strategies.

Strategy	*Score*
Uniformed patrol	16
Saturation patrol	16
Canine patrol	15.5
Presence of civilian transit personnel	15.5
CCTV	14
Plainclothes patrol	9
Decoy operations	9
Improved lighting	8.5
"Open" design	8

Source: D. Jacobson, L.G. Richards et al., AGT System Passenger Security Guidebook

Conclusion

Transit crime, particularly urban transit crime, is a major public concern. The majority of urban transit users and the general public perceive many transit systems to be crimeridden and therefore dangerous. In the case of New York City, crime in the subways actually accounts for only about 3 percent of total reported crime. The public perception of high crime rates in spite of this fact makes it incumbent upon transit police leaders and transit operators—in New York and elsewhere—to embrace strategies which address these perceptions and the resulting fear they cause. Public perception should be considered a major indicator of the quality of police service delivery.

While no strategy for coping with transit crime can be effective in all situations, a combination of strategies and security measures can be devised for maximum effect. The police executive and his management team along with transit operators need to develop and implement strategies which not only result in higher rates of arrest but also address and correct negative public perceptions. The strategies which appear to have the greatest benefit in the terms of the riding public are uniformed, saturation and canine patrol, the presence of civilian transit personnel, and CCTV systems. Transit systems and their police agencies should consider integrating these strategies into their total enforcement posture in a coordinated and careful manner. Special emphasis must be placed on coordinating operations with other police agencies, particularly other transit agencies and general service police agencies with which jurisdictional boundaries are shared.

Cooperation and coordination among agencies is necessary to combat criminal activity which transcends these boundaries. Without cooperation, the delivery of police service becomes fragmented. This fragmentation inhibits effective policing, which in turn benefits criminal activity. Careful attention must be given to strategies which displace crime. Strategies must be adopted in concert with other agencies to "capture" any displaced criminal activity. Without cooperative and coordinated police action between agencies, the needs of the public are given a low priority. Only through such cooperation and coordination can police agencies — transit or otherwise — address the needs of the public.

It is impossible to concretely recommend any single crime abatement strategy for transit crime due to the lack of quantitative research. Similarly, difficulties are inherent in statistically isolating the most effective factors in any multipronged approach to combatting transit crime. However, informed assumptions can be made concerning the utility of various strategies. Careful analysis, program evaluation and flexibility facilitate the application of cost-effective police response. Together with the elements of cooperation and coordination among police agencies and transit operators, analysis can provide the transit police executive with useful tools for the enhancement of passenger safety and security both on and near the transit system.

Endnotes

1. L. Siegal *et al., An Assessment of Crime and Policing Responses in Urban Mass Transit Systems,* National Institute of Law Enforcement and Criminal Justice, Law Enforcement Assistance Administration, U.S. Department of Justice, Washington,

D.C. April 1977 (Mitre Corporation: Mitre Technical Report No. MTR-7497, NILECJ/LEAA No. 76-NI-99-0111).

2. John P. Sullivan, "The Consolidation Issue: The Merger of Police Services in New York City" (Master's paper, The New School for Social Research, New York, 1986).

3. Editor's note to Phill Hickman, "Transit Crime and Policing," *Transit Policing* (Vol. 2, No. 1, Summer/Fall 1992).

4. E.J. Thrasher and J.R. Schnell, "Scope of Crime and Vandalism on Urban Transit Systems," *Transportation Research Record #487: Crime and Vandalism in Public Transportation.*

5. American Public Transit Association, *Transit Security Guidelines Manual* (Washington, D.C., 1979).

6. "Merger of New York City Police Agencies Creeping Off the Drawing Board," *Law Enforcement News,* 13 May 1985.

7. Larry G. Richards and Lester A. Hoel, "Planning Procedures for Improving Transit Station Security — Final Report," University of Virginia Department of Civil Engineering, Charlottesville, VA (Washington, D.C.: U.S. Department of Transportation, Research and Special Programs, 1980).

8. John Palmer Smith (unpublished research, New York Citizens Budget Commission, 1985).

9. James B. Meehan, "From the Desk of Chief James B. Meehan," *Around the Clock: New York City Transit Police Department News* (November–December 1985).

10. Jan M. Chaiken, Michael W. Lawless, and Keith A. Stevenson, *The Impact of Police Activity on Crime: Robberies on the New York City Subway System* (New York: The New York City Rand Institute, The Rand Corporation, 1965).

11. Ibid.

12. National Institute of Law Enforcement and Criminal Justice, *Policing Urban Mass Transit Systems,* p. XIV.

13. Richards and Hoel, "Planning Procedures."

14. Ibid.

15. Chaiken, Lawless, Stevenson, *Impact of Police Activity on Crime.*

16. New York *Times,* 5 February 1983.

17. Samuel G. Chapman, *Dogs in Police Work: A Summary of Experience in Great Britain and the United States,* Public Administration Service (Brattleboro, VT: Vermont Printing).

18. Ibid.

19. Richards and Hoel, "Planning Procedures."

Chapter 3

ON THE WATERFRONT: MARITIME, PORT AND CARGO SECURITY

With water forming nearly three-fourths of the earth's surface, it is not surprising that the waterborne movement of people and goods has historically shaped all aspects of the global economy. Ships, barges, ferries and boats have plied the world's oceans, seas, rivers, lakes, bays and bayous throughout the ages. So dynamic has the contribution of maritime commerce been to the economic health of nations, that river and seaports have traditionally been the hub of national life. Unfortunately, crime also has a long association with ports and maritime trade. Seafaring nations have a history of forming navies, coast guards and port police to ward off piracy, smuggling and cargo theft.

While the advent of railways, motor transport and aviation has shifted some of the commerce and movement of people away from the waterfront, vessels and ports remain vital elements in the transportation matrix.

According to Kenneth Hawkes,[1] maritime security concerns can be grouped into three major areas: vessels, ports and off-shore oil platforms. Other security professionals have identified theft, drug smuggling, sabotage, piracy, hijacking and stowaways as key contemporary maritime security threats. Seaport security responsibilities associated with these threats must protect the ships which call at a particular port, the cargo and the seaport itself.[2]

The Scope of Maritime Commerce and Security

Maritime trade and waterborne commerce are major components of the global economy. Because of the economic value of these goods in transit, their protection and security is essential. The following tables illustrate the importance of maritime commerce. *Table 3: U.S. Waterborne Foreign Commerce — 1992, Port Ranking by Cargo Value, Imports-Exports Combined* ranks U.S. ports by the value of their import-export cargo. *Table*

3-2: U.S. Waterborne Foreign Commerce—1992, Port Ranking by Cargo Volume, Imports-Exports Combined ranks U.S. ports by the volume of cargo handled. *Table 3-3: 1992 North American Cruise Volume* describes the passenger volume and vessel calls/sailings at selected ports in Canada, Mexico and the United States. *Table 3-4: 1992 Port Container Traffic* details the volume of containers shipped through selected U.S. ports.

Table 3-1. U.S. Waterborne Foreign Commerce—1992 Port Ranking by Cargo Value, Imports-Exports Combined (Millions of Dollars, 000s Omitted).

Rank	Port	Value
1	Los Angeles	$62,969
2	New York/New Jersey	55,072
3	Long Beach	50,428
4	Seattle	26,879
5	Houston	25,020
6	Oakland	24,124
7	Tacoma	22,950
8	Hampton Roads	19,481
9	Baltimore	16,862
10	Portland (OR)	15,407
11	Charleston	14,320
12	Miami	13,888
13	New Orleans	12,698
14	Savannah	11,452
15	South Louisiana	11,205
16	Jacksonville	8,850
17	Philadelphia	6,626
18	Port Everglades	5,104
19	Port Huron	5,089
20	San Francisco	4,395

Note: Rankings are for waterborne foreign commerce and do not include domestic cargo movements between U.S. ports. *Source: U.S. Bureau of the Census.*

What issues must a police agency address in order to effectively secure seaports and associated maritime facilities? Clearly, there is the security of the port itself—its terminal buildings, cargo handling facilities, docks, piers and quays. Next, there are the vessels which use the port. Vessels fall into three major classes: cargo ships, passenger ships (including ferries) and service vessels (such as tug boats, pilots, work boats). Finally, there is the cargo which is carried aboard and handled at the port.

A review of one agency's activity for one year helps to frame the context in which port police operate. Consider Ports Canada Police, the

Table 3-2. U.S. Waterborne Foreign Commerce—1992 Port Ranking by Cargo Value,
Imports-Exports Combined (Short Tons, 000s Omitted).

Rank	Port	Volume
1	South Louisiana	92,762
2	Houston	72,058
3	Hampton Roads	67,310
4	New Orleans	48,772
5	New York/New Jersey	42,242
6	Corpus Christi	36,277
7	Baton Rouge	34,236
8	Long Beach	29,163
9	Baltimore	25,842
10	Philadelphia	25,474
11	Port Arthur	25,281
12	Lake Charles	25,067
13	Los Angeles	23,429
14	Texas City	23,391
15	Mobile	19,907
16	Pascagoula	19,436
17	Tampa	17,983
18	Portland (OR)	16,314
19	Christiansted	14,201
20	Seattle	13,828

Note: Rankings are for waterborne foreign commerce and do not include domestic cargo movements between U.S. ports. *Source: U.S. Bureau of the Census.*

national port police agency responsible for protecting the ports of Vancouver, Montreal, Quebec, St. John's, Saint John and Halifax. The following table briefly describes their activity for 1992.

These incidents provide a glimpse into the types of activity a port police agency must address. Clearly, many of the concerns dealt with by general service agencies are present. Additionally, duties specific to a marine, cargo handling environment must also be taken on—cargo theft and drug trafficking, for example, are key maritime police concerns. Ports Canada Police recovered $174,606 (Canadian dollars) worth of cargo, while $417,126.86 (Canadian dollars) worth of cargo was reported stolen in 1992. In the same year, Ports Canada Police seized $59,325,830 (Canadian dollars) worth of illicit drugs.

Other issues facing seaport police include emergency preparedness and response to hazardous cargo accidents, organized crime, maritime fraud, stowaway aliens and maritime terrorism. This chapter will address these issues in addition to drug smuggling, threats to offshore platforms,

Table 3-3. 1992 North American Cruise Volume (Canada/Mexico/United States; Cruise Vessel/Revenue Passenger Traffic by Selected Ports).

Country/Port	Revenue Passengers	VesselCalls/Sailings
Canada		
Vancouver	449,239	54
Quebec	41,141	121
Montreal	36,147	236
Mexico		
Cozumel	619,660	477
Ensenada	353,549	589
Vallarta	268,463	263
Cabo San Lucas	259,826	284
Mazatlan	254,945	241
Acapulco	114,303	109
United States		
Miami (fy)	3,095,487	1,485
Port Everglades	2,279,918	1,571
Port Canaveral	1,082,221	555
St. Thomas (VI) (fy)	1,203,209	1,119
San Juan (PR)	1,128,565	1,773
Los Angeles	888,828	435
New York	310,969	189
Juneau	295,000	288
Honolulu (fy)	88,241	n/a
New Orleans	36,859	288

Abbreviations: fy = fiscal year
n/a = not available
Note: These ports are selected from a table provided by the American Association of Port Authorities (*AAPA Advisory*, May 3, 1993); statistics include port calls as well as traffic generated by homeported cruise ships.
Source: AAPA telephone survey and port records. Mexican data provided by Puertos Mexicanos; *AAPA Advisory*, May 3, 1993.

and the coordination of vessel and port security. An overview of shipboard security concerns is also provided.

In-depth discussions of issues related to maritime security are also found in other chapters within this text. Drug trafficking is examined in detail in Chapter Six: Illegal Drugs in Transit. Marine terrorism and passenger screening issues germane to passenger vessel security are addressed in Chapter Five: Transportation Terrorism. The issues surrounding emergency preparedness and hazardous materials incidents are discussed in Chapter Seven: Hazardous Cargo in Transit. Similarly, many of the issues concerning policing passenger ship terminals are

**Table 3-4. 1992 Port Container Traffic—Selected U.S. Ports
(TEUs/Metric Tons, Except Where Noted).**

Port	TEUs	Metric Tons
Los Angeles	2,289,038	n/a
Jacksonville (fy)	3,550,000	2,713,606
New York/New Jersey	1,970,161	n/a
Long Beach (a)	1,829,457	33,959,329
Seattle	1,151,261	8,057,000
Tacoma	1,054,449	6,708,801
Oakland (a)	1,234,150	16,521,100
Hampton Roads	846,256	5,981,158
Miami (fy)	519,954	3,724,513
New Orleans (b)	181,134	3,050,911

Abbreviations: fy = fiscal year

n/a = not available

TEU = Twenty-foot Equivalent Unit

Notes: (a) Metric Revenue Tons

(b) Boxes of varying lengths

Source: American Association of Port Authorities.

Table 3-5. Ports Canada Police—Activity and Incidents—1992.

Violent Crimes	68
Property Crimes	695
Cargo Thefts	193
Traffic Enforcement	2,582
Drug Enforcement	82
Small Vessel Regulations	368
By-Law Enforcement	829
Assistance to Canada Customs (Smuggling)	76
Assistance to Immigration Canada	158
Fatalities	46
Assistance to the General Public	662
Demonstrations/Protests	32
TOTAL INCIDENTS	5,790

Source: 1992 Annual Report, Ports Canada Police.

identical to those faced in policing public mass transit systems and their
terminals (see Chapters 2, 8 and 9).

Organized Crime on the Waterfront

A casual review of this century's newspapers and popular literature reveals a long-standing association between the waterfront and organized crime. So entrenched is this view that violence and racketeering are ingrained in the public perception of ports and their activity. In part this is due to the legacy of labor unrest and unfair labor practices which provided fertile ground for exploitation by organized criminal enterprises.

Without labor to unload them, cargo ships are no more than floating crates. Quick unloading and reshipment of cargo makes dockside labor an essential ingredient of the shipping process. Organized crime recognized this need and its concurrent potential for graft.

"In the worst days of the New York Waterfront—till the beginning of the 1950s, say—the complexity of the industry offered marvelous opportunities for graft."[3] At all levels of the dockside hierarchy, patronage was offered or withheld. Longshoremen had to "pay up" to get work; corrupt union officials demanded pay-offs from steamship companies to forestall work stoppages. Racketeers were given key positions from which they could "organize highly profitable systems of pilferage. . . . Rackets abounded, violence was commonplace."[4]

The cornerstone of this traditional organized crime dominance was the notorious "Shape-up" system, essentially a kickback racket. In order to secure a job on the docks, a longshoreman would have to kickback 10–20 percent of his wages to a hiring foreman. In order to be able to afford this payment, members of a longshore crew would frequently have to borrow funds from loan sharks. The loan sharks were usually associated with the same criminal enterprise and lent money at usurious rates. When the longshoreman was unable to pay back his loan, he was given a choice: participate in pilferage or hijacking, or become the victim of mob-sponsored violence. So successful was this endeavor that "in 1948 alone, the Grace Steamship Line reported losses of $3 million in pilfered goods, of which 80 percent occurred on its New York piers. Along with the losses on the docks, many trucks moving cargo between the piers and inland freight terminals were hijacked by armed robbers."[5]

By 1951 the spectre of organized waterfront crime was a national concern. The Kefauver Committee found that racketeers were "firmly entrenched along New York City's waterfront." These findings led to the New York Crime Commission hearings on organized crime at the port.

These hearings discovered that nearly one-third of union officials on the waterfront had criminal records, indicative of ties to organized crime.

As a remedy to this criminal entrenchment, an unprecedented body with broad legal, regulatory and police powers was established to route out organized crime and reform the docks. This body—the Waterfront Commission of New York Harbor—was established in 1953 to combat organized crime at the bi-state port of New York and New Jersey. Formed in response to an intensive investigation into organized crime and racketeering at the port by the New York Crime Commission in collaboration with the New Jersey Law Enforcement Council and local police agencies, the Waterfront Commission formed the cornerstone of efforts to restore public and commercial confidence in the vital port.

The compact (between the states of New York and New Jersey, approved by Congress) authorizing the Commission instituted a comprehensive framework for eliminating racketeering and corrupt practices at the port. The compact banned the pier "shape-up" which "enabled mobsters to control the employment and livelihood of pier workers."[6] The compact also banned "public loading," a practice which required truckers to make payments to groups of persons to load or unload cargo from their vehicles. These services, often accomplished through coercion and extortion, were required of truckers regardless of actual need.

The Waterfront Commission of New York Harbor today is constituted as a bi-state public instrumentality with broad investigative, licensing, regulatory and police authority over piers and terminals in the 1,500 square mile New York/New Jersey port district. Its major tasks are to:

- investigate criminal activity
- register/license longshoremen, stevedore companies, hiring agents, pier superintendents and pier guards
- regulate and monitor dock employment
- exercise broad police authority, including the issuance of subpoenas, conferring immunity from criminal prosecution, and the promulgation of rules and regulations.

Waterfront Commission Police focus their efforts on the investigation of criminal activity and conduct background checks of prospective licensees and registrants. Supporting this effort are detectives, investigators and waterfront intelligence analysts who collect, interpret and maintain organized crime data, and survey and evaluate the cargo protection facilities of stevedores and shipping lines. This unique agency monitors the entire port of New York and New Jersey, which embraces over 200 separate municipalities with an immediate consumer market of over 15 million persons. In 1990, it handled over 5,000 ship arrivals, contributing an estimated regional economic benefit of approximately $18 billion. In doing so, the port moved the equivalent of 1,210,170 20-foot cargo containers accounting for 48.9 million long tons (a long ton is 2,290 pounds) of oceanborne cargo, with a value of $50.233 billion.[7]

To achieve its mission, the Waterfront Commission actively monitors port employment. Persons or entities scrutinized by the Commission include:

Longshoremen: dockworkers employed to physically move waterborne freight;

Checkers: specialized dockworkers engaged in the checking or custodial accounting of cargo and clerical duties;

Pier Superintendents: persons employed by carriers or stevedores to supervise longshore and checker work;

Hiring Agents: persons who select dock laborers for employment on behalf of carriers and stevedores;

Telecommunications System Controllers: management or labor board employees who facilitate dockworker hiring via telecommunications;

Stevedores: entities licensed and authorized to engage in the movement of waterborne freight and to provide services incidental to such movement (e.g., cargo storage and container repair).

The Table 3-6 summarizes the number of registrations and licenses authorized by the Waterfront Commission in 1991.

Table 3-6. Waterfront Commission of New York Harbor Registration and Licenses—1991.

Longshoremen	5,129
Checkers	1,200
Hiring Agents	173
Pier Superintendents	278
Pier Guards	391
Stevedore Companies	68
Telecommunications Systems Controllers	14

Source: 1990–1991 *Annual Report,* The Waterfront Commission of New York Harbor.

The Waterfront Commission provides a unique case study for agencies or ports looking to contain organized criminal activity, particularly traditional organized crime, or to regulate port personnel. The organized crime threat to ports and maritime interests is dynamic, however, and new variations are emerging. Foremost among these trends is the growth of global organized crime. Analysts of this phenomena[8] note that traditional, fixed organized crime hierarchies are giving way to entrepreneurial enterprises which are suited for specific criminal tasks. Among these tasks are thefts from shipments, auto thefts and drug trafficking. This criminal specialization allows greater flexibility, resulting in enhanced efficiency and operational effectiveness.

Within this context, global organized crime can be described as either transnational or international in nature. Transnational organized crime involves criminals based in one nationstate who cross international borders to commit crimes and then return home. Common transnational crimes include auto theft, thefts of consumer goods from warehouses and shipments, and the illicit transshipment and dumping of hazardous wastes. International organized crime involves ongoing criminal enterprises with organizations and operations based in more than one nationstate. Included in this category are the Sicilian Mafia, the Japanese Yakuza, Chinese Triads and South American drug cartels.

Writing in *CJ International,* David L. Carter notes that organized crime groups find cohesion in various commonalities such as ethnicity (Triads, Tongs, Yakuza); geography (Sicilian Mafia, Calabrian 'Ndrangheta, Neapolitan Camorra); market ability (i.e., the ability to obtain, distribute and merchandise a particular commodity such as drugs, stolen vehicles, etc.); and sociopolitical outlook (e.g., outlaw bikers). All of these groups and their activities are of concern in the maritime port and cargo security context. Consider a unique example of geographic organized crime—piracy on the high seas. Carter points out, "Off the coasts of Southeast Asia, West Africa and Northeastern South America, organized crime groups of pirates have been involved in thefts. Typically, freighters are attacked and portions of the cargo stolen, along with the contents of the ship's safe, which frequently holds substantial amounts of cash to pay the crew and meet incidental expenses while underway. In a number of instances, the ships are steamed to another location, perhaps for several days until the cargo can be off-loaded. Not only is there a direct loss of goods and cash, but also an indirect cost of an estimated 6,000 pounds ($9,900) per day in ship operating costs."[9]

Not as exotic, yet equally alarming, are emerging trends in illegal commodities trading. European police report that both Eastern and Western European organized crime groups are extensively involved in the global trafficking of consumer goods and cars. "In particular," Carter observes, "the cartels trafficking in stolen vehicles have become very sophisticated, taking orders for luxury and sports cars. Many of these stolen vehicles end up in the Mid-East and Japan, after being transshipped through Northern Africa, where counterfeit registration papers and certificates of origin are prepared."[10]

Similar activity has been observed in Southern California, where international organized crime groups have been recruiting local gang members for carjacking and smuggling operations. An investigation into a highly publicized carjacking where a motorist driving a luxury car was murdered uncovered a link between vehicles being stolen—and, increasingly, carjacked—and Asian organized crime groups. A Los Angeles *Times* article recounting the trend pointed out that these vehicles were stolen or carjacked, then crated and shipped via freighter to China. Implicated in this activity is the Wah Ching, a domestic Asian crime group linked to the Hong Kong-based Triads. Local Asian street gang members are being recruited by the Wah Ching to provide the muscle for this lucrative trade. In the first eight months of 1993, this activity has escalated to the point where U.S. Customs officials have instituted enhanced monitoring of shipments from the Los Angeles area to the Orient. This monitoring netted $4 million worth of intercepted stolen vehicles during the same period.[11]

This type of activity illustrates the impact of global organized crime in the maritime, port and cargo context. It also serves to emphasize the link between crime in the community at large and crime at seaports. Organized crime in both traditional and emerging forms is attracted to the waterfront because of the access to ports, cargo and vessels and the opportunities for plunder which they provide. Due to this link, seaport police must anticipate organized crime incursions into their operational arena and formulate effective countermeasures, including intelligence capabilities and strong liaison with external police agencies at home and abroad.

Related to organized crime is maritime fraud. Fraudulent endeavors in the maritime, port and cargo context can be the result of individual or group action. Because of fraud's complexity and potential for income generation, however, the possibility of organized crime involvement should be kept in mind. Many types of fraud can be effectively conducted within the maritime environment. Four major classes will be discussed here: document fraud, scuttling/arson/insurance fraud, illegal reshipment/ diverted cargo, and charter fraud.

Document fraud typically involves the sales of nonexistent cargo and the substitution of cargo. Scuttling, arson and insurance fraud occur when a cargo is insured for high value. The ship or cargo is then destroyed in order to obtain insurance payments. Ships destroyed by fire or sunk in an area where retrieval is difficult are typical varieties of this fraud. Similarly, insured cargo—with a low value, vis-a-vis a ship—is dumped overboard, ostensibly to save a ship during a storm or other emergency situation.

Illegal reshipment/diverted cargo involves the illicit movement of hazardous waste or strategic goods, such as weapons, weapons-grade transuranic substances and the like. Diverted cargo entails the illicit diversion of legitimate cargo to a different port for illegal sale.

Charter fraud typically involves the collection of freight and shipping fees from persons or parties interested in moving goods, then not chartering a carrier while keeping the fees.

Each of these frauds can be conducted as a single act or in concert with other fraudulent activities. The victims of these types of maritime fraud include cargo owners, vessel owners and carriers, banks, insurance companies, and consumers. Port police can play a vital role in investigating these activities and making their tenants aware of such fraudulent endeavors, as part of their total service package. Similarly, port police can lend vital expertise to local agencies in their area in the conduct of fraud investigations involving maritime issues.

Another issue concerning port police and organized crime is drug trafficking and smuggling. Narcotic smuggling is a major international business utilizing all means of international transport, including cargo containers, vessels, crews and passengers. Because of the role seaports and marine facilities can play as a conduit for illicit narcotic smuggling, port police must remain aware of this threat and adopt appropriate countermeasures. Vessel owners and their masters must also place a high priority on containing this threat and thwarting unauthorized, illicit use of their vessels for this purpose. This need assumes particular relevance when the possibility of substantial fines and/or seizure of the vessel due to inadequate steps to counter drug trafficking aboard a vessel is considered.

While Chapter 6 focuses on this issue in depth, pertinent excerpts from the "Guidelines on Cooperation Between Customs Administrations and Ports Aimed at the Prevention of Drug Smuggling"[12] are reviewed here. These guidelines are intended to enhance cooperation between customs and port administrations throughout the world regarding efforts to detect and curtail narcotic trafficking and smuggling through ports. They advocate increased security aimed at reducing illegal access to and usage of port facilities, vessels and cargo (including containers) for the purpose of narcotic smuggling.

Among the guidelines are recommendations for port facilities to:

(1) Advise the appropriate customs agency of vessel movement (including arrival and departure) at the earliest opportunity;

(2) Facilitate enhanced access to movement information from the commercial sector (including changes in destination, consignees and special handling instructions);

(3) Provide prompt notification to customs authorities of unusual or suspicious documentation or activity;

(4) Provide cross training of customs officers in port container and cargo tracking systems; and

(5) Place a heightened emphasis on controlling illegal access to cargo.

Adoption of these measures on a uniform basis by ports worldwide would assist in the management of drug smuggling reduction efforts and enhance the overall level of security at ports.

Cargo Theft and Security

Cargo theft and security is a major issue which confronts police at seaports and, indeed, police responsible for protecting all modes of transportation. While focusing on cargo security at seaports and marine terminals, this chapter also reviews the impact of cargo theft on motor transport and railways since cargo theft impacts all modes of transport. "[It] disrupts the reliable and efficient flow of goods from shippers to receivers. It is also expensive; theft-related losses, which include the direct cost of the stolen cargo, higher insurance premiums, and additional administrative expenses, reduce transportation industry profits and increase prices for consumers."[13]

Losses experienced as a result of the theft of cargo in all transport modes are significant, yet their full extent is unknown. In 1979, a conservative estimate of direct costs due to cargo theft in the United States was $1 billion. Direct costs by mode were estimated at:

Motor carriers	$870 million
Maritime	80 million
Rail	41 million
Air	7 million

Indirect costs, such as filing, investigating and paying claims, were believed to be two to five times that amount.[14] Current levels are generally believed to be at least at the same volume.

While no central clearinghouse collects, collates or reports cargo loss data, pilferage—that is, the theft of partial loads—or cargo theft—the theft of full loads—appears to be stable or slightly on the rise. In fact, certain types of theft, such as hijacking and truckjacking, appear to be on the increase in certain regions. In 1991, for example, the Los Angeles County Sheriff's Department reported 244 thefts of full trailers or containers valued at $27.4 million within their jurisdiction alone.[15]

Other factors also highlight the potential extent of cargo theft. While containers help to limit pilferage, they provide an attractive target to thieves, providing convenient one-stop shopping. "Much larger 'packages' containing higher value cargoes could now be spirited away with comparative ease and the spoils made it worth using more elaborate methods of deception and daring. Whereas, previously, ten televisions might go missing because that was all the thieves could carry or secrete, now two hundred could be stolen at a go in a container."[16]

Other analysts agree, pointing out that "after an initial honeymoon period, during which criminals adjusted to the new (container) system, other patterns of theft developed."[17] Indeed, this is a worldwide trend, with container industry analyst Barry M. Tarnef noting that "theft of containers from storage or marshalling facilities or on the road are not unusual in the United States, Italy and Nigeria."[18]

Containers are increasingly the standard mode of moving cargo along all transit modes. First used by military traffic commands to reduce pilferage of supplies and materiel, containers were extended to commercial usage in the mid-1960s. Wide acceptance was ensured by their benefits in operating efficiency. Goods could be handled in less time utilizing fewer personnel. The majority of containers in use are standard box size or twenty feet long, hence the TEU or twenty foot equivalent unit; although at least fifty separate specialty containers of various lengths are also in use worldwide.

After an initial drop in losses due to the shift from bulk shipping ("break bulk"), cargo loss in the containerized environment appears to be on the rise. Some experts, such as Barry M. Tarnef, feel losses now equal or exceed the levels prevalent during the break bulk era.[19] The actual dollar loss, however, is hard to calculate. Shippers and insurance companies are reticent to report loss to police authorities which could publicize theft and inhibit customer confidence. "Theft-related losses are 'a cost of doing business.' Good security measures, such as adding fences and guards, checking seals, and counting cargo as it is loaded and unloaded, can be expensive. As a result, industry often views it as less costly to absorb the smaller claims and have insurance cover the larger claims."[20]

Additional rationales for underreporting include:

(1) Carriers frequently fear shippers may shift business to another carrier due to security concerns;

(2) Carriers want to limit the ability of competitors to disclose their security record as part of efforts to gain market share;

(3) Fear that insurance companies will use theft statistics to justify increased premiums for coverage; and

(4) An inability to pinpoint the actual point of loss during a complex journey.

While underreporting obscures the full extent of cargo theft, some trends appear to be developing. Key among these is the increase of violence associated with theft. In Los Angeles, which is increasingly viewed as the cargo theft capital of the world—the combined ports of Los Angeles and Long Beach provide an attractive target since they form the largest cargo handling network in the world—gunmen recently shot a security guard and stole two tractor-trailers containing clothing and merchandise valued at an estimated $1 million.[21] Such incidents are not isolated.

Another trend is the movement of theft and hijacking from seaports and marine terminals to surrounding highways and roads. Improvements in port security have led perpetrators to seek the softer target, making cooperation among local and seaport police a renewed priority. Similarly, increased global organized crime involvement in illicit cargo shipments and transnational activity is evident (e.g., an estimated 30–50 percent of cargo stolen in the Los Angeles region is diverted to Mexico).

Containers can be stolen as a whole, opened and made subject to pilferage, or serve as a conduit for narcotic smuggling. A good understanding of containers, therefore, is essential to combatting cargo theft.

The majority of containers in deep-sea or international use are registered with the Paris-based *Bureau international des containers (BIC).* This international nongovernmental organization serves as a clearinghouse for documenting container ownership and registry codes. The BIC has accordingly grouped required customs, safety and regulatory codes and identification markings into a single, documentary BIC Code.

Containers are also marked with additional data such as a customs approval plate, a safety compliance mark (Container Security Convention), technical specifications, and an owner's symbol. Weight data is also affixed to each container, generally beneath the BIC Code. The BIC Code, due to its universality and internal numerical integrity, is perhaps the most important sentinel to police officials regarding potential fraud.

The BIC Code is located at the top right aspect of the container door as follows:

BIC Code Exemplar

ICSU   405230 3
USA   2210

where each segment represents:

| owner's code | designated serial number | check digit |
| country code | size and type code | |

The weight table below the BIC Code denotes:

maximum gross weight
tare
maximum payload.

As previously discussed, in the precontainer environment pilferage was the primary method of stealing cargo. Now a range of activity prevails. Theft ranges from "shopping" (i.e., opening a container to remove specific items, often by removing seals then resecuring the container, or removing doors and then taking the cargo) to the theft of entire containers, often by hijacking (driving a tractor-trailer up, loading the container and driving away through fences or with the use of fraudulent papers) or by using force, such as a truckjacking.

It is important to note that a large proportion of cargo and container thefts involve persons within the cargo/shipping industry. "Well over 80 percent of all theft and pilferage of transportation cargoes is accomplished by, or with the collusion of, persons whose employment entitles them access to the cargo that is stolen."[22]

Recognizing the potential impact of cargo theft on the national economy, particularly on the transportation industry, the U.S. Department of Transportation through the Office of Transportation Security has recommended that industry develop standards to cope with key cargo security issues. Among the issues identified are the need for procedures addressing:

(1) Seal accountability
(2) High value commodity storage
(3) Internal accountability
(4) Cargo loss reporting, and
(5) Pilferage high-value or sensitive cargo transit.[23]

Cargo terminal security is an important element of a comprehensive effort to combat cargo theft. Seaport police or other agencies involved in protecting cargo in transit should be aware of the ingredients needed to develop an effective terminal security program, which should be designed and implemented by the terminal operator. Three major steps are involved in developing such a program:

(1) Determine an acceptable level of loss.
(2) Conduct a site security survey.
(3) Select and implement a security program.

While determination of an acceptable level of loss, and selecting and implementing a particular security policy or program are policy issues to be evaluated by terminal management, essential aspects of a site security survey can be stated here. The following outline summarizes key elements to be considered during such a survey.

Figure 3-1. Site Security Survey.

A. PERIMETER
  Fencelines
  Entrances/access point
  Docks, moorings
  Lighting
  Alarms/CCTV
B. INTERIOR/FACILITY
  Container traffic volume
  Container types (wheeled, grounded, mixed) and mix
  Roll-on/roll-off volume
  Railhead interface
  Freight consolidation
C. CARGO STORAGE
  Layout
  Traffic patterns
D. BUILDINGS

Figure 3-2. Continued

Guard shacks
High-value cribs
Document storage
Computer facilities
Support facilities (locker rooms, kitchens)
Private vehicle parking
E. **EXTERNAL OPERATING ENVIRONMENT**
    1. Port Characteristics
      Ships handled
      Volume
      Road, rail, waterfront access
    2. Port Administration
      Port management
      Port police and security
    3. Local Characteristics
      Local police support
      Local crime conditions

When conducting a site security survey, it is important to walk around the facility, review maps and site plans, and talk with the people who work there. Valuable insight into how to bypass or contravene existing procedures to gain illicit access can frequently be gained from persons most familiar with the facility.

The perimeter is the facility's first line of defense against unauthorized entry and possible theft. Fencelines, entrances and access points—including docks and moorings—should be surveyed. Current lighting, alarm systems and surveillance devices should be assessed and tested.

After examining the perimeter, the interior of the facility itself should be reviewed. The present volume and type of cargo or container traffic should be noted, and past and projected activity should be assessed. The specific quantity of activity and its type are important determinants in the selection of appropriate security measures. Does the facility handle only container traffic? Is bulk cargo also processed? What is the main product moved through the facility? Is there a railhead interface? Is freight consolidated? These types of questions are important.

Next, how is the cargo stored? The layout of storage areas and traffic patterns through the facility should be examined. Potential procedural weaknesses which facilitate easy access, and any insufficient monitoring should be noted. Where are buildings located and what is their function? How could a thief use them to his or her advantage?

Once the facility is examined, consideration should be given to the external operating environment and its impact on the terminal. Is it a port or inland facility? If it is a port facility, what types of ships are handled? How many over a day, week, month? Is there access to the terminal and surrounding port infrastructure by road or rail from the waterfront?

Finally, what type of port or governmental support mechanisms are available? Does the port management actively support security efforts; does it have programs in place to assist tenant terminal operators? Is there a port police or security agency, and what is their mission and/or focus in relation to this specific terminal? What local crime problems, such as gangs, organized crime, etc., are likely to impact the terminal? What local police resources are available to counter these problems and support this cargo security effort? An accurate assessment of these dimensions will aid in the development of options for a site-specific security plan.

Access control lies at the heart of any terminal's security program. All vehicles and individuals entering or leaving the cargo facility should be monitored. Similarly, parking areas should be controlled and segregated from active cargo areas.

Physical measures usually form the basis of any terminal security program. Foremost among physical measures is fencing. Fences should be in good repair (fabric taut, attached to uprights), anchored to the ground, and have barbed wire with outward facing angle irons and/or razor wire at the top. Fence alarms and closed circuit television (CCTV) monitoring may be considered as an adjunct to unencumbered visual scrutiny of the fence line by security personnel. Reinforced fence lines should be considered to thwart vehicular fence breeches. Fences can be reinforced by placing linked K-blocks (Jersey barriers) or I-beams linked with cable inside the fence.

Access points and gates are critical links in the perimeter. Active gates should be monitored by security personnel. Unused gates should be sealed, and any gate not in active use should be locked. All access traffic should be consolidated whenever possible. The use of gate alarms, CCTV monitors and barriers—such as calthrops or dragon's teeth—which can be activated and retracted when necessary should be considered. Key and pass control are essential.

Lighting is likewise a vital element of a site security program. Four main types of lighting are available: continuous lighting, which provides overlapping total coverage; standby lighting, which is activated only during periods of suspicious activity; movable lighting, such as searchlights, which are generally used to supplement the above two types; and emergency lighting, which is used as a backup source of illumination during emergencies. Optimally, a mixture of each of these types of lighting will be deployed on a site-specific basis. Additionally, each of these types can be projected in one of two ways, either as glare projection or controlled lighting.

Glare projection lighting projects a wall of light, creating a "barrier" which makes it difficult for a potential intruder to see past. It illuminates persons outside the facility while providing an element of concealment within. This type of lighting is typically seen in a police setting when officers illuminate vehicles with their spot lights during traffic stops at night. Controlled lighting simply illuminates the area (e.g., a street light). The type of light source should be selected on a site specific basis after careful consultation with a security lighting specialist.

Careful selection of security personnel is another element of an effective security package. Security officers can be either proprietary or contract employees. Regardless of the source, quality personnel are essential. Screening and pre-employment background checks should be conducted whenever possible. Registration of security personnel, as in the Waterfront Commission model, should also be considered. Appropriate levels of supervision and training should be provided. Finally, detailed post orders detailing essential tasks and expectations should be developed, and knowledge of these post orders should be a mandated element of job knowledge for all security officers. Regular, formalized interaction with port and local police should be encouraged.

Container seal discipline, seal security, container storage, and inventory control are the final elements of a comprehensive terminal security program. Cargo seal discipline is vital. "Cargo seals are the least expensive means of deterring theft. They provide 24-hour protection from point of origin to destination, no matter what the distance or time span. A good seal control system is also a good investigative tool, as it pinpoints where the theft occurred (between what two points the seal was tampered with or broken)."[24]

Container or cargo seal discipline for a cargo terminal should entail detailed inspections with recorded checks noting the seal number, date, time, place of exam, and container number at arrival and departure from the terminal, during stacking, during relocation within the terminal, during loading/discharge from a ship, and during the opening of container doors for customs or drug enforcement checks. During customs or drug enforcement checks, the container should be immediately resealed once the check is complete and all pertinent details noted. New seals should also be attached whenever a seal irregularity is detected or suspected.

Typical seal irregularities include no seal, a damaged seal, or a substitute seal. The attachment of a supplemental "security seal" should be documented and appropriate transport and investigatory agencies (i.e., port police, cargo theft investigators) notified. Random checks of container seals should be considered as an effective countermeasure to seal tampering, with high value cargoes receiving heightened scrutiny, including frequent logged patrol checks.

Seal security is an important subcomponent of seal discipline. Unused seals must be secured in a locked cabinet and access to them must be restricted. Seals should only be issued for specific uses. When issued, issuance should be recorded. Attachment of seals should only be conducted by supervisory personnel, and not by workers engaged in cargo handling.

A variety of cargo seals are currently available, including a strap or band seal; twist-seal wire; cable seal; 5$\frac{1}{6}$ inch carriage bolt and nut; bullet or rod-type high security seal; adjustable lock (i.e., an enforcer security lock); rear door hasps—roll up locks; and fiber optic seals. Cargo theft investigators and port security personnel should become familiar with these seal types, along with their common applications and relative merits.

Finally, under certain circumstances it may be desirable to implement security oversight of seal handling procedures. When storing containers, grounded (nonwheeled) containers should be stored door-to-door. No unsealed containers should be allowed in a storage area and all private vehicles should be restricted from entering the storage and cargo handling areas. No persons should be allowed in the storage area without prior, preferably written and recorded, authorization.

Inventory control is the final element of a cargo security program. All container and cargo activity at a given terminal should be tracked. In order to do so effectively, chassis numbers must be correlated with license (tag) numbers on wheeled vehicles to facilitate police detection and recovery in case of theft. Tracking and monitoring is particularly important for high value goods. All high value cargo should be subject to additional scrutiny and supplemental security (i.e., locks, monitored storage, frequent patrol checks).

Documentation is the key to inventory control. To be effective, documentation must occur—at the very least—at terminal entry and exit. Documentation at terminal entry includes logging the driver and delivery papers, and is enhanced when entering and exiting containers are separated. Exit documentation should preferably involve a two-step process. An excellent example of this dual release procedure is provided in *Terminal Security,* a guidebook on cargo security measures developed by Through Transport Mutual Services.[25] A simplified explanation of the two-step or dual release procedure is as follows: When a trucker arrives at the terminal entry gate, he presents his documents to the gate controller who then issues a yard pass and gives the trucker pick up instructions. The controller retains a copy of the pass, and container release is authorized. The trucker picks up the designated container and proceeds to the exit point. At the exit point, the documents are crosschecked with the container. The chassis number is recorded. Release is confirmed. A release form is prepared and signed by the driver and also the exit controller or clerk, and a copy is retained by each. Optimally, a photo of the driver and the front license plate of the tractor-trailer is also taken at this point. The vehicle is then allowed to exit the cargo facility. Adopting such a container retrieval and release process minimizes fraudulent, unauthorized release of valuable containers.

Another element of terminal security centers around any rail and terminal interfaces. As intermodal containerization increases in prevalence, container freight security at rail links can be expected to become more important. While "frequent minor theft is the main security risk faced by container freight stations ... effective cargo segregation, tallying and seal discipline is needed."[26] Cargo and container security at rail links requires these additional steps.

The sheer bulk of most rail container cargo precludes much theft of full loads, since specialized handling equipment is needed. Nevertheless, high value items and other portable goods require scrutiny to prevent minor theft and pilferage. It is imperative that import and export cargo be segregated and seal discipline, as well as cargo handling monitoring, be maintained. Empty containers should be stored apart from cargo loads. Containers should be loaded on rail cars with their doors blocked (i.e., door-to-door) to prevent access. Port police should also maintain a high level of cooperation with railroad police special agents, sharing information concerning theft trends. Port police should routinely advise railroad police whenever a high value cargo such as small consumer goods is being shipped through the port to inland distribution points, especially when the cargo must travel over congested inner city rail lines subject to frequent stops—the perfect site for potential "box car burglary."

In addition to terminal security measures, a number of general cargo theft countermeasures can be articulated. Primary among these is prevention and target hardening, especially as concerns high value loads. Among the strategies available are a high security presence, convoys, low-profile movement and vehicle tracking technology.

High security presence can be achieved by frequent marked patrol presence along heavily travelled arteries in and around terminals and in areas which have experienced significant hijacking or truckjacking activity. Patrols can be provided by marked police or security vehicles. A variation on this strategy has been employed by Zenith Electronics Corporation, which has assigned two truckers per rig to minimize opportunity for theft.[27]

A unique variation on high security presence has been used in the form of intensive saturation operations in Jersey City, New Jersey. Jersey City is a major urban center within the New York/New Jersey port district. Trucks moving within the port often utilize local streets since main arteries in the city are frequently congested. Criminal groups have capitalized on this traffic by diverting trucks carrying consumer electronics into dead end streets and cul-de-sacs, then mobbing the trailer to pilfer goods. Employing a classic sting operation, Jersey City Police have posed as tractor drivers with additional officers hidden in the box of the truck to apprehend perpetrators when the theft occurs. Jersey City Police have widely publicized these efforts through the electronic media to dissuade potential criminals.

Another high profile security measure is the convoy, or convoys and concentration (con-con). In this method, which is reminiscent of World War II North Sea convoys, high value shipments are grouped together and travel with radio access to police support or direct security escorts. The U.S. Postal Service has used this technique to successfully reduce hijackings of mail trucks and bulk shipments.

Low profile movement is another way to protect valuable shipments. In this low cost method, trucks or containers hauling high value goods are plainmarked—that is, they travel without the display of corporate logos advertising desirable contents to potential thieves. Attention to contents is diverted, and thieves seek more attractive bounty.

Vehicle tracking technology provides the fourth means of target hardening. Electronic devices such as Lo-Jac, Teletrac or other tracking equipment can be located in containers or on-board trucks in order to facilitate rapid recovery—often within minutes—in the event of a reported theft.

Police intervention can also be an effective countermeasure to cargo theft. Both specialized port police and local police agencies have an interest in deterring cargo theft and detecting violators. Careful attention should be given to developing unilateral and/or multijurisdictional cargo theft and suppression teams. Multijurisdictional teams may prove especially effective in terms of results and fiscal efficiency. They can be configured to involve port police, local police agencies, and railroad police, and can integrate participation from pertinent corporate security agencies.

The following team management issues should be considered when developing a multijurisdictional cargo theft investigation and suppression team. First, team mission and objectives must be clearly stated. The proper multijurisdictional mix must be developed, with clear reporting and operational methodologies adopted and endorsed, preferably through memoranda of understanding among all participating agencies. Dedicated prosecutorial support is a definite plus. If possible, a fulltime deputy district attorney or prosecutor should be secured. This capability will ensure quality search and arrest warrant preparation, and ensure adequate prosecutorial follow-through of potentially complex investigations which require significant expertise and detailed case preparation.

Statistical and data analysis are essential. A dedicated crime analyst skilled in interpreting and collating both reported incidents, field interview reports and intelligence summaries can effectively isolate trends and help to direct valuable investigative efforts.

Fiscal oversight and reporting for undercover operations and issues related to managing confidential informants must not be overlooked. Careful prescreening of team members and close attention to integrity control are of obvious importance.

Issues related to logistics such as evidence management and the vouchering of recovered property cannot be understated. An effective cargo theft suppression team will, by necessity, have to marshal the support services needed to process large quantities of often bulky and valuable merchandise. Sufficient secure storage areas and specialized equipment and operators must be available at a moment's notice.

Electronic surveillance capabilities are also valuable assets for supporting this type of operation. Team members should have access to this equipment, be able to use and repair it, and be able to describe its use in detail if called upon to do so in court.

Public-private partnerships can be considered as a way to increase the utility and effectiveness of cargo theft investigation and suppression efforts. The whole range of corporate entities—including cargo, transportation, warehousing and insurance industries—along with national, state, local and transportation police agencies all have a stake in and expertise to lend to cargo security efforts. Technical assistance, information sharing and financial and logistical support of investigations can be undertaken by such a partnership.

Public-private partnership should also include a commitment to prevention and recovery activities. Corporate entities must accept the responsibility to accurately report cargo thefts and share information with police. Consider the success of the California Trucking Association's "Hijack Alert" program. Utilizing fleet drivers on the lookout for stolen rigs, 52 out of 53 trucks reported hijacked in 1991 were recovered.[28] The only information necessary to sustain this program is an accurate reporting of hijacked equipment identification numbers (i.e., tractor, trailer and container chassis and license numbers, VINs or vehicle identification numbers, and container BIC Code numbers).

Finally, attention must be given to developing the skills necessary for coordinating interagency operations. All port and local police departments involved in cargo theft investigations and security must develop these skills in order to facilitate effective multiagency coordination, cooperation and communication. Frequently, all that is needed to achieve this end is interagency dialogue and preplanning, including joint training and exercises. By combining these efforts, port and local police can develop meaningful measures to counter the growing cargo theft problem.

Maritime Terrorism and Piracy

Acts of aggression and violence directed against merchant vessels at sea seem exotic at first glance, recalling a past era of pirates and clipper ships. Historically, piracy was robbery on the high seas. Armed ships plied the waters of the Barbary Coast and the Caribbean and South China seas engaging merchantmen to gain plunder. Armed private ships known as privateers were commissioned by governments to attack warships of rival nations, engaging in an early form of proxy warfare, and acting as a predecessor to modern maritime terrorism.

Both maritime terrorism and piracy are plausible modern threats. Far from being exotic, modern piracy actually thrives in many parts of the world today. Until the highly publicized *Achille Lauro* incident, maritime terrorism was not a high priority concern. Many terrorist groups themselves avoided conflict at sea, perhaps lacking technical skills in shiphandling and navigation. Foremost among the reasons for avoidance of engagement in the marine arena was a fear "that their maritime operations would be inherently vulnerable to swiftly moving naval forces. This fear turned out to be unfounded. Naval forces are quite helpless against the seizure of ships and hostages at sea."[28] Indeed, the sea and maritime interests provide ample targets for terrorists, particularly state-sponsored terrorists. Targets "range from economic targets, such as offshore oil-drilling rigs, to massive human targets on passenger liners or ferryboats . . . includ[ing] the ecological disaster of oil tankers disgorging their cargo."[29]

While marine terrorism may not have been a high profile issue, it has not been unknown in the last three decades. Quasi-terrorist incidents such as bombings and bomb threats have also been directed against maritime targets. Analysts of maritime threats have catalogued several significant events of this type.[30] Examples include the October 1960 bombing of the New York City ferryboat *Knickerbocker,* the January 1961 hijacking of the Portuguese cruise ship *Santa Maria,* where 560 passengers were held hostage for eleven days, and the March 1973 sinking of the cruise ship *Sanya* by a limpet mine in Beirut.

In January 1974, Japanese Red Army and Popular Front for Liberation of Palestine (PFLP) terrorists teamed up to set fire to a Singapore oil refinery, hijacking a ferryboat to facilitate their getaway. Later that year, guerrillas from the Moro National Liberation Front (MNLF) seized the Philippine ferry *Don Carlos,* and took hostages. Three years later in October 1979 the MNLF hijacked the Malaysian vessel *Haleha Baru Adel,* killing at least 44 passengers. The Irish Republican Army (IRA) has operated in the marine environment, placing bombs on passenger ferries in February 1972 (*Duke of Argyle*) and July 1974 (*Ulster Queen*). In November 1976, the IRA attempted a bombing against the *Queen Elizabeth II.* In February 1981 the *Nellie M.,* a collier, was boarded and sunk by the IRA.

Perhaps the most notorious maritime assault in recent memory was the October 1985 hijacking of the *Achille Lauro,* where passengers were held for two days. This event resulted in the death of a passenger, Leon Klinghoffer, and created widespread governmental awareness of the threat of terrorism at sea. This was not, however, the last incident of note. In July 1988, the cruise ship *City of Poros* was boarded and assaulted by submachine gun-wielding terrorists who killed nine and injured 47 persons.

Samuel Menefee, an observer of maritime terrorism, has noted that ¼ferries appear more vulnerable than other passenger vessels based on activity to date. "In all cases, arms appear to have been smuggled aboard, presumably in luggage, suggesting that adequate monitoring may pay dividends in reduced attacks."[31]

Piracy is the second major threat against maritime interests. As noted earlier, piracy is defined as robbery on the high seas. Under U.S. law, codified at 18 USC 1652, the definition of piracy has been expanded to include murder and other acts of hostility. The section states,

> Whoever, being a citizen of the United States, commits any murder or robbery, or any act of hostility against the United States, or against any citizens thereof, on the high seas, under color of any authority from any person is a pirate, and shall be imprisoned for life.[32]

Far from being a historical curiosity, piracy and pirates are currently active in the Caribbean, throughout the South China Sea, and along the coasts of West Africa and Latin America. Between 1982 and 1985 pirates in the Gulf of Thailand killed at least 388 refugees, abducted 587, and raped 734. An additional 967 refugees are missing and presumed dead. Shipping lanes such as the Strait of Malacca and the Phillip Channel are notorious among merchantmen as hotbeds of piracy. Tankers and cargo vessels sailing the Phillip Channel must be on the lookout for fast boats carrying grappling hooks and armed pirates, since these vessels are prime targets for boarding and assault.

The combined threats of terrorist assault and piracy make vessel security an extremely important priority. Like maritime security at port, access control is the key. Vessel security is dependent upon vigilance and adequate access control. Masters of vessels should make shipboard security a high priority and should appoint an officer to the position of security officer. Essential aspects of vessel security are discussed in depth in Kenneth Hawkes's excellent text *Maritime Security*. Hawkes reviews the threats vessels face including pilferage, stowaways, drug smuggling, sabotage, piracy and hijacking. The need for standard shipboard operating procedures detailing actions to be taken against specific hostile threats cannot be understated.

Masters and security officers must ensure the development of vessel security plans based on comprehensive, up-to-date security surveys. These plans should include standard operating procedures for responding to threats according to the vessel's operating status, including:

moored dockside
moored dockside/cargo handling
at anchor
at anchor/cargo handling
underway·
rendering assistance at sea
docking/undocking
receiving and discharging pilots
receiving ship's stores
bunkering
receiving official visitors and guests
changing crew.[33]

These procedures should utilize physical security measures such as lighting (both glare projection and controlled lighting) and specialized lighting (e.g., high-powered strobes to confuse and hamper intruders such as nighttime underway boarders). Similarly, the ship's layout should be used to foster tactical advantage to crew during security alerts or mobilizations. Priority should be given to protecting critical areas such as the bridge, radio room and engine room from intrusion.

Consideration should be given to activating perimeter patrols and static observation posts tailored for each operational mode. Patrol staffing should at a minimum include specific deployment models for each of the ship's major modes (i.e., at port, moored alongside pier or wharf; at anchor; or underway). Additionally, the development of a shipboard reaction force with set protocols for action depending upon operational mode is strongly encouraged.

Crew skills and response capabilities should be honed and tested through regular immediate action drills. Three major classes of drill should be developed, in ascending order of magnitude:

(1) Disturbance or suspicious activity
    —on pier or in vicinity of vessel
(2) Intruder(s) attempting to board
    —from pier
    —while at anchor
    —while underway
    —while rendering assistance at sea
    —while receiving or discharging pilots
(3) Intruders on board.

Each major class should be drilled at regular intervals. A progressive exercise program can be developed, starting from the least complex and low-risk situations (disturbance/suspicious activity) and progressing to the most complex and high-risk situations, as the crew gains competence and confidence in their protective and defensive capabilities.

Finally, the master and security officer of each vessel need to develop and maintain high levels of cooperation through regular liaison with port police and security officials at each port of call. Vessel and port security must be closely integrated to effectively limit the risks faced both at port and underway.

Related to vessel and port security is the security of offshore platforms. "Although there have been few reported attacks on offshore platforms, the array of threats is quite diverse."[34] All maritime facilities, including offshore rigs, could be targeted by guerrillas and terrorists, conventional criminals, environmental extremists, and hostile employees.

In 1981, British and Norwegian antiterrorist units were placed on alert following a credible warning by persons believed to be linked with Palestinian terrorists that a North Sea oil installation was targeted for terrorist action. British authorities take threats to these facilities seriously, especially in light of their economic vitality. Accordingly, the elite Commachio group of the Royal Marines counts antiterrorism and protection of North Sea installations among their priority tasks.

Terrorism analyst Brian Jenkins categorizes the potential hostile actions which could be directed against offshore platforms as bomb threats; bombings; mines; boardings and armed assaults; stand off attacks; remotely piloted vessels or aircraft; manned vessels or aircraft; off-site antipersonnel attacks; occupations or hostage-barricade scenarios; traditional sabotage and theft of equipment. These threats are similar to those faced by all maritime entities, including port facilities and vessels at port or underway. Port police should consider these as possible threats which may be directed against their facility and develop appropriate contingency action plans.

While actual assaults against offshore installations are possible, Jenkins discounts them as a present high level target, stating "although offshore platforms seem vulnerable targets, theoretically attractive to a diverse group of potential adversaries, the actual history of criminal activity involving platforms does not support an assessment that the threat is high."[35] He does acknowledge the possibility that this could change as the number of offshore sites increases, making them more accessible, or as the result of technological or political developments.

Piracy and terrorism are two real threats facing the entire maritime sector. Passenger vessels, particularly cruise ships, are especially vulnerable to threats related to terrorism since they move numbers of people in a nonrestrictive atmosphere. Broadly speaking, cruise ship security involves three aspects: terminals, shipboard and outports. Access control, once again—particularly the monitoring of gangways, passengers, crew and baggage screening—is essential.

International Maritime Organization resolution A-584(14), "Measures to Prevent Unlawful Acts Which Threaten the Safety of Ships and the Security of Their Passengers and Crews" articulates standards for governments, port administrators, ship owners and operators, the masters of vessels, and crews to strengthen port and vessel security in light of the threat of maritime terrorism. These issues are discussed in depth in Chapter 5 and draw from the experiences of the civil aviation community which are discussed in Chapter 4.

Alien stowaways are another issue impacting the maritime community. Stowaways and concerns related to alien smuggling can be expected to remain sensitive issues as long as economic and political stresses stimulate the movement of people from impoverished areas to industrial or postindustrial nations which promise migrants an improved quality of life. Port police need mechanisms for cooperating with immigration authorities and handling large numbers of alien stowaways fairly and humanely pending action by immigration authorities. Port police must remain aware of possible organized crime involvement in alien trafficking. This is often manifested in extortion and virtual kidnapping of aliens, who are held in poor conditions as indentured servants by unscrupulous racketeers seeking ransom from the alien's relatives at home to end their *de facto* captivity. Linkages with public health authorities and victims' services agencies, along with the capability to impound the vessel and detain its master and crew, need to be arranged in advance for this eventuality.

On a smaller scale, legitimate ship owners, operators and masters need to develop methods for preventing the introduction of alien stowaways to sovereign nations. In the United States, ship owners, masters and officers are subject to fine if they provide a means for unauthorized alien entrance to the country. This makes the prevention of stowaways and detection of unauthorized persons attempting to come aboard, or the detention of unauthorized persons once they have come aboard, a prudent course of action. Once alien stowaways are aboard, they must be prevented from exiting the vessel and gaining illegal entrance to the port of entry.

Herman Gomez, a Miami Port Police official with expertise in this area, recommends the following steps for coping with alien stowaways.

(1) Ships should be checked for stowaways at the port of origin prior to departure.
(2) Ships should be rechecked by crew once underway.
(3) All crew should be aware of the consequences of transporting stowaways and maintain a high level of onboard awareness.
(4) Detention facilities (i.e., secure holding areas) should be available on all ships for the detention of stowaways pending transfer to appropriate authorities.[36]

Finally, coordination of vessel and seaport security is essential. Steps for ensuring such coordination require an exchange of seaport and vessel security plans among all appropriate authorities; a high level of security awareness; relevant security training; and an emphasis on access control. A coordinated approach to these issues both within the seaport and with all vessels utilizing the seaport is the only way to address the complex security and crime control concerns addressed in this chapter. A high degree of professional competence combined with interagency, interdisciplinary cooperation is required to secure seaports, vessels, persons working in or travelling through ports, and cargo from these multifaceted threats.

Endnotes

1. Kenneth Gale Hawkes, *Maritime Security* (Centerville, MD, Cornell Maritime Press, 1989).

2. Herman Gomez, Kenneth Hawkes, *et al.,* "Securing the World's Seaports," *Security Management* (June 1992).

3. Jan Morris, *The Great Port: A Passage Through New York* (New York: Harcourt, Brace & World, Inc., 1969).

4. Ibid.

5. T.J. English, *The Westies: The Irish Mob* (New York: St. Martin's Press, 1990).

6. The Waterfront Commission of New York Harbor, *1990–1991 Annual Report.*

7. Ibid.

8. See "The Status of Global Organized Crime: Reflections from an International Meeting at the Police Staff College at Bramshill" by David L. Carter in *CJ International* (Vol. 9, No. 5, September/October 1993).

9. Ibid.

10. Ibid.

11. Vicki Torres, "Foot Soldiers Add Violent Twist to Asian Street Gangs," Los Angeles *Times,* 15 August 1993.

12. See "Guidelines on Cooperation Between Customs Administrations and Ports Aimed at the Prevention of Drug Smuggling" by the Customs Cooperation Council and the International Association of Ports and Harbors, November 1989 for comprehensive guidelines for ports administrations and customs authorities regarding the suppression of narcotic smuggling.

13. U.S. General Accounting Office, *Report by the Comptroller General of the United States: Promotion of Cargo Security Receives Limited Support* (Washington, D.C.: 31 March 1980).

14. Ibid., Office of Transportation Security estimates as reported in Comptroller General's report.

15. "Cargo Theft on Rise in L.A. Area: One of the Easiest, Most Lucrative Crimes for the Risk," *Transport Topics* (No. 2978, 31 August 1992).

16. Roy Campbell, "Study in Crime," *Cargo Systems* (May 1991).

17. Barry M. Tarnef quoted in "Security of U.S. Ports Challenged by Thieves, Smugglers and Terrorists" by Carlos J. Salzano in *Traffic World* (25 September 1989).

18. Ibid.

19. Tarnef, quoted in "Security of U.S. Ports," *Traffic World.*

20. U.S. General Accounting Office, *Report by the Comptroller.*

21. Eric Malnic, "Robbers Kill Guard, Steal 2 Big Rigs and $1 Million in Goods," *Los Angeles Times,* 2 September 1993.

22. United States Department of Transportation, *A Report to the President on the National Cargo Security Program* (Washington, D.C.: 31 March 1980).

23. For additional information, see cargo security advisory standards included in Part 101-1 through 101-5 of Title 49 of the Code of Federal Regulations (49CFR101-1 through 101-5).

24. Robert L. Coy, "Theft Investigations in a Seaport," *Maritime Security Manual,* Seaport and Harbors Subcommittee of the Standing Committee on Transportation Security, American Society of Industrial Security (1990).

25. Through Transport Club, *Terminal Security* (London: Through Transport Mutual Services, 1992).

26. Ibid.

27. Rebecca D. Russell, "Secure Transport From Here to There," *Security* (Vol. 27, No. 3, March 1990).

28. *Transport Topics* (No. 2973, 31 August 1992).

29. Yossi Snir, "Maritime Terrorism," in *Future Terrorism Trends,* Yonah Alexander, Yuval Néeman and Ely Tavin, eds. (Washington, D.C.: Global Affairs, 1991).

30. Ibid.

31. See "Terrorism, Extortion and the Cruise Industry" by Samuel P. Menefee in *Maritime Security Manual,* American Society for Industrial Security, and *Maritime Security* by Kenneth Gale Hawkes (Centerville, MD: Cornell Maritime Press, 1989).

32. Menefee, "Terrorism, Extortion and the Cruise Industry," *Maritime Security Manual.*

33. Title 18, United States Code, Section 1652.

34. See *Maritime Security* by Hawkes, particularly Chapter 4, "Security Measures and Procedures."

35. Brian Michael Jenkins, "Potential Threats to Offshore Platforms," *Terrorism, Violence, Insurgency Report* (Vol. 8, No. 2, 1988).

36. Ibid.

37. Herman Gomez, "Foiling Alien Stowaways," *Maritime Security Manual,* Seaport and Harbors Subcommittee of the Standing Committee on Transportation Security, American Society of Industrial Security (1990).

Chapter 4

AIRPORT CRIME

Eclipsing the seaports, railway stations and bus terminals of past generations, the airport now serves as a focal point in modern transportation. By 1989, 450 million passengers had boarded 6.5 million flights at U.S. airports alone, checking in 700 million pieces of luggage annually. Passengers and cargo shippers alike rely on the swift transit provided by air carriers. Early in aviation history airports were usually located in isolated areas, remote from the pressures of urban life. With the growth in air transit and its related support services, however, criminals have discovered a fertile venue for a variety of illegal activity.

Twenty years ago airport police were viewed as little more than custodians. Aviation-directed terrorism, hijacking and transnational crimes such as drug trafficking and arms smuggling have changed that role. Responding to these challenges as well as to the wide range of traditional policing concerns, airport police agencies have come to the forefront of the battle against crime. Indeed, airport police contingents are often larger than many small to medium sized general police service agencies. New York's John F. Kennedy International Airport provides a striking example. Law enforcement personnel at JFK include the 225 uniformed and 28 detective members of the Port Authority of New York and New Jersey Police, 400 U.S. Customs officers, as well as agents from the Drug Enforcement Administration, the Immigration and Naturalization Service, the Secret Service and the Federal Bureau of Investigation. In addition, each airline has its own security staff. The interplay of these separate agencies—each with its own operational methods, philosophy and goals— requires skillful planning and coordination. Cooperation is essential in tackling the problems encountered in the aviation environment.

Modern airports are complex intermodal transport centers housing numerous activities. The average daily population of many airports rivals that of a medium-sized city. Runways, terminals, hangars, warehouses, high risk security storage areas, container stations, truck depots, car rental businesses and their vehicle storage areas, parking lots and many other services such as gas stations, banks and restaurants create an infrastructure quite vulnerable to crime.

Airport police today must confront such disparate problems as the purse snatcher and the organized crime drug runner. Traffic enforcement, auto thefts and burglaries, ticket fraud, homeless persons seeking refuge in terminal facilities, the threat of terrorism—all combine to form the challenge to airport law enforcement agencies.

Cargo/Baggage Theft

Cargo and baggage theft are among the most costly of airport crimes. Of 27.2 million passengers at New York's JFK International Airport in 1986, for example, 1,500 passengers reported stolen luggage with a corresponding loss of approximately $3 million.[1] Cargo theft losses, including the appropriation of gold, jewels, furs, electronic equipment and the like, far exceed that figure.

In addition to the direct costs incurred by carriers, property owners and insurance companies, cargo and baggage theft can have harsher indirect costs to both the airport operator and the region at large. A high rate of cargo theft at a particular airport may influence an airline to divert its airfreight to another nearby airport. The reduced volume of airfreight, through a reverse economic multiplier effect, can lead to a downturn in the region's economic health.

When developing a strategy for coping with cargo theft, airport managers and police note that as on-airport security increases, theft tends to shift to cargo handling and storage facilities located off-site. Close coordination with the adjacent police authority and commercial security and loss-of-assets divisions is necessary. Involving airport-based police in the development of crime prevention programs for surrounding business interests is a useful tactic, providing positive public relations as well as ensuring the airport's position as a cargo handling facility.

Labor racketeering and organized crime are closely related to both baggage and cargo theft. This connection is reflected by the evidence that a good number of airport crimes are "inside jobs." For example, many thefts occur inside a plane's cargo hold after airport and airline employees have used X-ray machines to screen for valuables as well as security risks. The sophistication and complexity of much of this crime, as well as the past incidence of organized crime involvement, makes organized crime a real threat to airport operations.

Local organized crime families, supported by their connections with factions of organized labor, have often staked criminal business opportunities in and around airports. An active intelligence capability combined with cooperation in ongoing organized crime mitigation efforts is required if airport police are to effectively combat these activities.

Related to cargo theft is mail theft. Air mail packages often contain gold, currency and other valuables. Effective management of mail theft requires ongoing coordination with postal security authorities. The increasing privatization of the postal sector as evidenced by package services such as Federal Express will require liaison with the private sector in this regard.

Contraband

The influx of contraband across international borders necessitates a close working relationship between airport police and various national customs and treasury agents. Munitions, counterfeit commercial products (imitation Rolex® watches, Louis Vuitton® handbags and similar items), currency, high technology equipment not licensed for export, and endangered wildlife are frequently found at international airports. The most notorious contraband, of course, is illegal drugs and narcotics.

Almost any container is suspect as a hiding place for narcotics. At Miami International Airport, for example, large shipments of carnations and other flowers often provide concealment for cocaine. Weapons and large sums of undeclared currency, often related to drug smuggling, are also encountered. Random searches and drug detection dogs are among the countermeasures used to deter this trade.

Airline personnel are frequently involved in transnational drug trafficking. In March 1987, for example, forty Pan Am, Eastern and Delta airline employees at New York's JFK airport were arrested and charged with conspiracy to smuggle several tons of cocaine worth $1.5 billion from Brazil since 1981. These workers apparently circumvented Customs officials by moving suitcases containing cocaine through crew areas not subject to search on a regular basis. A countermeasure which could reduce the likelihood of this type of crime as well as other security breaches is to subject airline personnel to baggage and weapons screening. This is now the norm in the United States as a result of the December 1987 downing of a PSA flight in California by a disgruntled former employee.

The March 1987 JFK arrests were unique, the successful result of the first time that local airport police and federal agents had combined efforts on an overseas assignment. In this case, Port Authority of New York and New Jersey Police assigned to JFK worked undercover with a federal agent in Brazil. This type of cooperative effort can be a useful tactic in the fight against transnational crime.

Auto Theft

Another problem increasingly encountered at airports is auto theft. Large parking lots, both short- and long-term, provide an opportunity for car thieves to practice their trade.

Auto theft in general is a serious problem for the law enforcement community. It is a low-risk, high profit crime which offers the thief (or often, group of thieves) a greater potential profit than robbery or burglary with a reduced risk of confrontation or apprehension. Professional thieves many times steal cars to order. The cars are then altered, given false documentation and resold in the "grey" market. Vehicles can also be cut up for parts in a "chop shop."

A common outlet for stolen cars is a "VIN switch." This refers to the changing or altering of a specific auto's vehicle identification number (or VIN). Each VIN has 17 characters, one of which is a computer-generated check digit which can be used to detect tampering. Every car produced has a VIN which is inscribed at several key places on that car. The easiest to locate is the "public VIN," the metal plate attached to the front left portion of the auto's dashboard. The public VIN is so located to facilitate observation by police officers. In fact, courts have determined that a police officer may enter a vehicle to relocate objects on the dashboard which obstruct the view of the VIN plate. (For additional information on the Fourth Amendment issue, see New York v. Class, L.Ed. 2d81 (1986).)

In addition, VIN plates are located in several other spots. Interested law enforcement officers can contact the National Insurance Crime Bureau (NICB), formerly known as the National Automobile Theft Bureau, Inc., to obtain detailed information. NICB produces motor vehicle identification manuals as well as a pocket-sized VIN location chart. Besides the public VIN plates, each vehicle also has a secret VIN whose location is made known only to police.

In a VIN switch, a stolen vehicle is reregistered with documents from a totaled vehicle of the same make, model and year. To carry out this action, a thief will purchase a badly damaged vehicle, steal a similar vehicle, remove its VIN plates, and replace them with the damaged car's plates. Having the owner's documents from the damaged car which correspond to the "new" VIN on the stolen car, the thief will then reregister the stolen car. Since badly damaged cars are often legitimately rebuilt, the thief hopes to pass off his crime as a genuine effort. Chop shops are organized entities that perform these VIN switches as well as dismantling stolen vehicles for sale as auto parts.

Another associated problem is the theft of car audio equipment, such as stereos, from vehicles parked in airport lots. In this case, high value autos with exotic sound systems are often targeted.

To effectively deal with the spectre of auto theft in airport parking lots, airport police need to be aware of the current trends in auto theft. Local police agency auto theft investigators are a good source of information, and cooperative efforts can produce greater results. Parking lots should be patrolled regularly in a nonroutine manner, with officers paying close attention to the signs of auto theft and tampering.

Terrorism

In addition to the conventional crimes faced on a regular basis, airport police must be ready to cope with the ever growing threat of terrorism and aircraft hijacking. The December 1988 bombing of Pan Am flight 103 over Lockerbie, Scotland, which killed all 259 people on board and 11 on the ground, renewed the scrutiny of airline security practices. To address these challenges, airport management and police must provide a high level of protection to airport facilities and aircraft in a manner which disturbs normal operations as little as possible. This is only possible through the corroboration and cooperation of the airport operator, airlines, the civil aviation authority, police, security services, labor unions, customs authorities and various civil authorities. This corroboration requires a preestablished organizational structure with a clear delineation of responsibilities.

Government authorities such as the Federal Aviation Administration (FAA) or Britain's Transport Ministry lay down security parameters but individual airline and airport security agencies must implement and enforce them. The experience of El Al, the national air carrier of Israel, may provide some important tactics for secure air travel. Passengers on all El Al flights are required to report to the airport two hours prior to scheduled departure time, where they are interviewed by El Al security agents and their luggage hand-searched and x-rayed. El Al agents ask specific questions about each bag, such as: To whom does the luggage belong? Who packed it? What presents or gifts are being carried? Who gave them to the passenger? Where has the bag been since it was packed? What is the passenger carrying that does not belong to him or that he does not know the contents of? In addition, at least two armed El Al security agents travel on each flight, and all planes are physically target-hardened.

In Rome, police monitor traffic entering the airport area and perform random physical searches at airport entrances. Passengers at check-in counters are interviewed by airport personnel and those fitting terrorist profiles are referred to police for further checks. Passengers must then pass through metal detectors and have their baggage examined and x-rayed. A final check occurs at the boarding gate where more random searches are conducted. Police then escort buses across runways and monitor boarding of aircraft. Parked planes are guarded, and armored cars escort planes while they taxi. Police helicopters are used to protect high-risk aircraft during take off.

Thorough knowledge of an airport maximizes security. The operational areas of an airport are divided into two designations, airside and landside. Airside includes the aircraft operations area—runways, taxiways—while the landside encompasses terminals, transit interface areas, ticket counters, offices and the like.

The airside must be considered the prime target for a terrorist attack against aircraft and, as such, must be secured. Fencing, identification of authorized personnel and vehicles, direct protection of aircraft, control of general aviation, and control of passenger flow from one area to another are among the methods used to protect the airside from intrusion. Fencing obviously helps to deter intruders by delaying and inhibiting unlawful entry and by controlling access to vulnerable areas.

Issuing and keeping track of identification keeps access restricted to authorized personnel. All ground crews should have passes limiting entry to specific areas on an at-need basis only. Airport police should issue and monitor the passes, which would include a photo and be tamperproof. Strict pass control, subject to periodic checks, could be supplemented by the use of color-coded vests. Specific colors could correspond to specific operational areas. This option allows visual control from a distance in addition to the pass checks. All vehicles which regularly travel airside should have a unique identification placard, and all occupants would be required to possess appropriate identification. Vehicles entering the airside on a nonregular basis would be issued temporary identification or be escorted, with escort the preferred method.

The protection of aircraft can be accomplished through the use of floodlights, the locking of aircraft doors, and removal of stairways from unattended aircraft. Staging areas can also be monitored by video cameras and physical patrol.

Controlling general aviation also enhances an airport's security picture. Aviation traffic should use separate, designated taxiways, ramps and parking areas, and the mixing of unsecured aircraft should be avoided. All general aviation taxiways and aprons would be subject to security checks.

The transfer of passengers, baggage and cargo is a critical link in any airport's security program. The transfer of incoming or outgoing traffic can pose a risk if the originating airport had lax security provisions. Also, if a plane's destination is located in a high-risk area, enhanced security measures are desirable.

The training, screening and supervision of x-ray and metal detector technicians and checkpoint security agents must be enhanced, along with security procedures related to baggage. It may be wise to eliminate curbside check-in or reconciliation of baggage, and to station security agents at check-in counters as well as at checkpoints. Bags could be marked after passing through security. These practices could be coordinated throughout an airport to provide uniform security for all carriers.

Since the Pan Am flight 103 bombing in Scotland, more attention has been paid to electronic devices. Semtex, a plastic explosive, was concealed in a cassette tape player on the fatal Pan Am flight. Passengers should be required to demonstrate that all electronic devices are operable.

The isolation of a compromised aircraft is essential should an incident occur. Aircraft involved in a terrorist assault, bomb threat or hijacking must be relocated to an isolated, secure area subject to surveillance and amenable to a range of possible countermeasures, including negotiation and counterassault.

As previously noted, the airside/landside boundary needs to be well defined with a clear delineation of "sterile," limited and controlled access areas. Passenger screening, including physical searches and x-ray/metal detector checkpoints, can aid in this endeavor, along with the use of explosive detection dogs and devices. Intensified searches of air crews and their baggage is recommended.

Cargo terminals must not be overlooked. Once again, staff identification, secured doors, windows and access points, the designation of high risk storage areas, and surveillance can help to secure these areas. It should be remembered that terminals with high levels of conventional crime are likely to have unsecured areas which can be infiltrated by terrorists.

As security tightens at airports traditionally plagued by terrorism, less protected airports become more inviting targets. Effective provisions for airport security essentially include fencing and manned barriers; alarm systems which provide intruder detection; lighting; checkpoints, including metal detectors, x-ray baggage screening devices (both portable and stationary), physical search, bomb detector dogs and mechanized bomb detection devices; pressure chambers for subjecting baggage to simulated flight altitudes to detect and explode pressure-activated explosives in a safe setting and bomb or explosive disposal capability.

Emergency Planning

Operational functions for airport policing include (1) the prevention of and response to conventional crime; (2) the screening of passengers, baggage, cargo and mail for contraband, explosives and dangerous devices; (3) security management for VIPs and special risk flights; and, of great importance, (4) the management of threatened or actual extraordinary events. These events might include a bombing, an assault to aircraft, facility or persons, or seizure of an aircraft in flight or on the ground, or a threat of such an action. Aircraft emergency planning is essential, and should encompass not only unlawful acts and terrorism but natural disasters, fires, aircraft accidents, and chemical, radiological and hazardous materials releases.

The airport police executive is responsible for the coordination of law enforcement measures and the activities of other concerned agencies. He or she must maintain liaison with external security and emergency services, airlines, airport operations and civil authorities. The military, customs, immigration and other police authorities as well as fire, rescue and emergency medical services, postal services, utilities and telephone companies, cargo and transportation entities all require his or her consideration.

Because of their potential for large numbers of injuries or deaths, aircraft accidents require special attention. The International Civil Aviation Organization (ICAO) divides aircraft emergencies into three categories: aircraft accident (on or in the vicinity of an airport), full emergency and local standby.

An aircraft accident requires that fire and rescue services be activated and dispatched to the incident. A full emergency exists when an aircraft approaching the airport is in trouble with the possibility of an accident forthcoming. In this case fire and rescue units are placed on standby at predetermined staging areas. A local standby occurs when an aircraft is experiencing trouble but should have no difficulty landing. Fire and rescue units are again placed on standby at predetermined staging areas when a local standby exists.

Regardless of the class of emergency, fire and rescue units should be able to respond to any part of an airport's operational area in no more than three minutes. A two minute or less response time is preferable since rapid response obviously maximizes potential passenger survivability in event of a crash. Effective response to aircraft accidents is enhanced by realistic preplanning, frequent incident drills and simulation, effective communications and coordination and cooperation among responding agencies. Airport police play a great role in achieving these goals, as well as their frontline duties: securing an incident perimeter, maintaining crowd control, securing personal property and emergency equipment, maintaining the integrity of an incident scene to preserve evidence and facilitate later investigation and the identification of injured and deceased passengers.

Conclusion

Airports are highly complex social and technological centers with populations often reaching that of busy urban cities. Airport police, in common with police at other types of transportation centers, are faced with the general nature of crime plus specific problems related to their environment. Policing an airport requires not only a solid knowledge of general law enforcement but an expertise in the special nature of airports and a willingness to coordinate action with a number of separate agencies. The vital mission of maintaining secure aircraft travel requires a cooperative spirit to ensure the performance of essential tasks.

A recent example of cooperative effort was spearheaded by the U.S. National Central Bureau (USNCB) of Interpol, the International Criminal Police Organization. As a response to the internationalization of crime and society in general, USNCB encouraged each state to develop a liaison point to facilitate requests for international assistance and cooperation. USNCB mandated that the organization chosen to function as this focal point must have both statewide investigative jurisdiction and 24-hour communications capabilities. Initiated in April 1987, thirty-six state liaison offices were in operation by February 1989, with the remaining states pursuing some stage of development or review.

As the liaison process developed, the USNCB noticed that airport and seaport police in many states were not operationally situated in such a way to allow them immediate access to the information the USNCB was generating. Recognizing this void and the particularly high potential for transnational criminal activity at airports and seaports, the Port Authority of New York and New Jersey Police encouraged officials of several major airports and USNCB personnel to meet.

One of the findings of the meeting noted that each individual airport had accumulated a wealth of information regarding the criminals and criminal organizations which target airports. Intelligence included information on such crimes as pickpocketing, cargo theft, drug trafficking, credit card fraud, money laundering and terrorism. Many of the organizations and individuals known to the police had followed distinct patterns in their criminal activities, and were known to migrate from airport to airport. Yet no formal mechanism existed for sharing this information.

The USNCB and Interpol have the capability to direct this information to airport and seaport authorities, as well as general police agencies. The USNCB liaison with airport authorities has currently been formalized as an adjunct to the state liaison programs under the name Airport Law Enforcement Agencies Network (ALEAN). The potential for this type of initiative is obviously great and may help to curb the growing ills of airports in an increasingly complex society.

Endnote

1. Roy Rowan, "How the Mafia Loots JFK Airport," *Fortune* (22 June 1987).

Chapter 5

TRANSPORTATION TERRORISM

Transportation facilities provide potential terrorists with highly visible symbolic targets which, when attacked, yield maximum effect and devastation. Vehicles in transit offer terrorists targets which are virtually impossible to secure. The persons likely to suffer the effects of terrorist assault directed against transportation facilities are innocent and usually removed from any implied political connection. Terrorist assault is a threat to public safety and security. The threat of terrorism is heightened when one considers the long-term implications of terrorist incidents on the orderly operation of a facility and the perceptions of the traveling public. Transportation operators and police need to recognize the threat terrorism poses and must plan for the rapid management of such acts, including the critical stress these incidents can place on normal operations and contingencies.

It is extremely difficult to secure many transportation facilities because of their public nature and high volume of usage. The constraints posed by these factors as regards security can create conditions quite attractive to potential terrorists. Despite these difficulties, transportation agencies and police can develop both proactive and reactive capabilities to minimize the potential effects of terrorist incidents by combining awareness, adequate planning and the development of intelligence and tactical response capabilities in cooperation with other agencies with thorough training and drills.

Preventive design and other security measures are essential to the safe operation of public transportation facilities and systems. Security can be provided through both physical means and by the use of a uniformed patrol force. However, both police patrol and physical security measures have limitations in deterring terrorist attacks. Without a clear threat or demonstrated emergency, it is doubtful that the public will accept the use of intrusive or inconvenient security measures. A real question also arises over the utilization of measures which demand unusual concessions in terms of individual privacy and free movement unless a demonstrable threat exists.

To cope with these limitations, organizational capabilities for developing an appropriate response to terrorist incidents must be used to the best advantage. Special training on all levels, identification of skills already existing within the ranks of the police, the deployment of specialized units and interagency cooperation can form the foundation for managing and deterring terrorism.

In addition to internal preparation, transport facilities must be prepared to cope with the impact of events originating off-system. Consider, for example, the February 26, 1993 bombing of New York City's World Trade Center. The bombing, which killed six persons and injured over 1,000, occurred in an underground parking area adjacent to the primary New York terminus of the bistate PATH commuter rail system. The ceiling of the rail terminal collapsed and debris was spread to the lower level platform areas as well. Provisions for extrication of trapped persons, involving urban rescue, care of injured persons, crowd control, monitoring of the system for secondary impacts, and mechanisms for joint incident resolution must be prepared.

In 1984 there were nine actual or attempted bombings of transportation facilities in the United States. Of these, six were actual bombings and three were attempts. Of the actual bombings, four involved explosives and two involved incendiary devices.[1]

Following is a discussion of the three major areas of transportation terrorism: marine, rail and aviation. We will also outline the evaluation of terrorist threats, contingency planning, interagency cooperation in planning, the need for intelligence gathering and the strategic and tactical management of transportation-related terrorist incidents.

Marine Terrorism

The 1985 *Achille Lauro* hijacking raised many questions about the integrity of security measures aboard ships and at ports. This concern is especially vital to the police of port authorities and the operators of seaports and marine terminals. In particular, the *Achille Lauro* incident heightened concern over the need for improved maritime security and highlighted the possibility that terrorist assault against maritime and seaborne targets may become part of the repertoire of international terrorism.

The *Achille Lauro* incident did not mark the first assault by terrorists or other criminal actors against seaborne targets. Between 1980 and 1984, some 400 cases of piracy or armed robbery of vessels have been identified.[2] Cruise liners, petrol tankers, ferries and cargo vessels have also been the targets of terrorist-initiated bombings and hijackings. Despite a history of terrorist assault against marine targets, international terrorism is predominantly land-based. The preference for land versus marine targets is probably due to the greater number and variety of land-based targets and the fact that many forms of maritime terrorism tend to require sophisticated equipment and elaborate logistical planning.[3] The greater quantity and variety of land-based targets combined with the need for sophisticated assault capability no doubt factors into decisions by terrorists to continue attacks against land-based targets such as government offices, airline offices, embassies and military installations.

However, with a worldwide increase in terrorism of between 12 to 15 percent[4] and the tendency for terrorists to seek new and exciting targets which guarantee continued media and public interest, terrorist groups may begin to view maritime targets as viable, attractive options. Beyond the public impact, ports and seaborne targets provide terrorists with the ability to negatively impact a nation's commerce, trade and economy. "A series of attacks against symbols of international travel could very well result in a reduction of international trade and commerce, just as recent incidents have adversely affected international tourism and travel."[5] Clearly, such impacts threaten a nation's vital interests and can affect national security. Such threats clearly illustrate the need for tighter port and shipboard security. To date, however, marine, port and vessel security is nowhere near as developed as aviation security. This is evidenced by the lack of uniform, codified marine security regulations of the type promulgated by the Federal Aviation Administration (FAA) for aviation facilities.

The security provisions of the Federal Aviation regulations were enacted after skyjacking began to have a deleterious effect on civil aviation. It is to be hoped that the maritime sector, reflecting on the positive experiences of the aviation security program, will "harden" its targets and enhance security measures before being forced into action by violent acts or passenger avoidance. As a result of the *Achille Lauro* affair, over 12,000 vacant accommodations for Mediterranean cruises have been estimated.[6] This impact has caused various governments and the United Nations-sponsored International Maritime Organization (IMO) to examine passenger ship and port security provisions. As a result of this examination, the IMO adopted Resolution A.584(14), "Measures to Prevent Unlawful Acts Which Threaten the Safety of Ships and the Security of Their Passengers and Crews." This resolution, adopted in November 1985, recognizes the serious threat of piracy and seaborne international terrorism, and calls upon "all governments, port authorities and administrations, ship operators, ship masters and crews to take, as soon as possible, steps to review and as necessary, strengthen port and onboard security." Interestingly, but not surprisingly, the IMO pointed to the experience of the International Civil Aviation Organization (ICAO) as a guide to aid in the development of practical technical security countermeasures. If the maritime industry is to follow the lead of its aviation counterparts, the major burden of security will fall on port facilities as opposed to individual vessels. If this becomes the model for passenger ship security, the boarding process for cruise ships will become similar to that of airlines. Passengers will walk through portal metal detectors, baggage will be searched or subject to scrutiny, and the traditional bon voyage of wellwishers coming aboard for a final goodbye will go the way of transatlantic steamships. Additionally, seaport police at passenger ship terminals will see their role become increasingly similar to their counterparts at airports. This possibility will require seaport police to closely examine aviation security procedures and modify them to fit the passenger ship/marine environment. Close cooperation and consultation with airport police will facilitate the task of securing marine terminals from potential terrorists.

While measures drawn from the aviation experience will be relatively easy to implement at passenger shipping facilities, the measures necessary for securing cargo vessels and terminals may prove more difficult. Since the threat to cargo does not generally raise the same level of public concern and outcry, industry support for securing cargo facilities may not be as great. Also, the unique physical arrangements of cargo handling areas—often open and away from public scrutiny—pose many difficulties in containment. Yet the threat of terrorist assault against cargo vessels and handling facilities is not diminished. Terroristic attack on cargo provides an opportunity to disrupt commerce and economic activity in a way which will not generate the loss of public support which often follows the casualties resulting from antipersonnel attacks.

The threat of terrorist assault against marine cargo is particularly high when considering the risks inherent in hazardous cargo shipments.

"European concerns about marine terrorism are not focused on passenger ships but on ships carrying hazardous and/or pollution cargos."[7] The potential environmental hazards which arise from an assault on hazardous cargo shipments in transit pose many difficulties for police and civil government, not the least being the engenderment of casualties or the need for evacuation. The special considerations encountered in this type of scenario are discussed in Chapter 7.

Regardless of the type of maritime terrorist or piracy incident, seaport police need to consider a variety of countermeasures and strategies. Robert G. Moore, a retired United States Coast Guard Captain, in his article "The Price of Admiralty: Regulatory Response to the Threat of Maritime Terrorism" suggests four factors which any program designed to cope with maritime terrorism must review. The first: roles of all levels of government—federal, state, local, port authorities and supranational—must be defined, and within this definition, assessments must be made and standards established. The second: security offices, officers and plans must be designated for each ship and port facility. Within this framework, regular assessments of capability and inspections of status are essential. The third factor: security programs must be comprehensive, including provisions for planning, training, essential equipment, and the elaboration of standard operating procedures. Finally, these programs must be flexible, with the ability to upgrade response or alert status according to the level of the existing threat.

These factors are in many ways similar to those found for response to other types of transportation terrorism and terrorism in general. As such, they are discussed only briefly here. Together with many of the strategies for coping with transportation terrorism discussed throughout this chapter, they can be combined in a way which will maximize police and governmental efforts to curtail maritime terrorism.

Rail Terrorism

Rail transportation systems, both rail passenger and rail freight, provide terrorists with visible, unsecured targets. Passenger systems (intercity, commuter and subways) provide highly visible targets which represent the authority of the government or of the established order, carry large numbers of people in an unsecured environment, and are susceptible to extensive disruption. Freight systems provide terrorists with easy to assail, unsecured targets which can disrupt economic activity and make a statement without yielding a large number of casualties or deaths which can compromise public support. Freight systems, since they transport large numbers of chemicals and toxic materials, provide terrorists seeking to escalate tactics the opportunity to create a hazardous materials incident which could be costly to contain and clean up, and which may require evacuation—ensuring maximum media coverage.

Historically, modern terrorists have sought vulnerable targets which would ensure media coverage. As society responds to these incidents by hardening potential targets through improved security measures, terrorists may seek the "softer" targets provided by a rail transit infrastructure. Urban mass transit systems are particularly vulnerable since they transport large passenger volumes and present an array of opportunities for disruption. Further, they are hard to secure because of their passenger volume and scope of operation.

Although rail terrorism has not been prevalent in the United States, foreign rail transit systems (as well as bus systems) have frequently been the focus of terrorist assault. During the three year period December 1983 to September 1986, there were 42 actual or attempted terrorist incidents directed against mass transit worldwide. Of these incidents, 7 were attempts, 2 were cases of civil disorder, and 33 were actual terrorist assaults. Of the actual terrorist assaults, 2 cases involved sabotage and 31 cases were bombing incidents (including multiple bombings and arson). Additionally, there was one case of shooting consequent to a bombing. Twenty-four of these assaults were directed against rail targets, 3 against buses, and 6 against terminals. Rail-directed assault had an incidence four times greater than terminal-based terrorism. Rail incidents occurred eight times more often than bus-targeted incidents.

These figures can be enlightening to the police administrator or transportation executive seeking to enhance system security and upgrade capabilities to defend against on-system terrorist assault. Rail targets demand greater attention, and in-service rolling stock is the most vulnerable to attack. To cope with these needs, right-of-way needs to be secured. Countermeasures which could harden right-of-way include perimeter fencing and lighting, and random aerial (helicopter) patrols of the area. Random vehicular patrols and vehicular access could also be useful in this regard.

Aviation Terrorism

Aviation-directed terrorism is the form of transportation terrorism which receives the most public attention. Of twenty terrorist incidents which occurred during the one year period April 1985 to April 1986, 35 percent were directed against airports, aircraft or airline offices. Threatened acts of terrorism against aircraft or airports are also in evidence. Between January 1 and June 30, 1982, 583 threats were directed against aircraft and airports. Of these, 461 were considered serious by the authorities in charge. These serious threats resulted in at least 159 searches and at least 98 delayed or diverted aircraft movements. One hundred twenty-two bomb threats resulting in 94 searches and 17 evacuations were directed against airports during the same time period.[8]

The Tables 5-1, 5-2 and 5-3 illustrate criminal activities of a terrorist or quasi-terrorist nature directed against U.S. civil aviation and the results of the U.S. passenger screening program during the same period.

Passenger screening is intended to detect firearms and explosive or incendiary devices which pose the greatest threat to civil aviation. In the United States, passenger screening is the responsibility of the air carriers. In Europe, screening is usually conducted by the airport authority or by the state. Air carrier screening is supported by airport law enforcement agencies. This support basically falls under one of three models:

Model A. Law enforcement officers are present at all screening checkpoints during all screening.

Model B. Law enforcement officers using overt and covert communications methods patrol the immediate checkpoint area while specially trained air carrier personnel conduct screening.

Model C. Law enforcement officers using overt and covert communications models patrol the terminal area away from the screening checkpoints together with increased training of air carrier screening personnel.

Model C is preferred of the three, since law enforcement officers are available throughout the terminal or airport area, providing a higher level of police visibility and allowing greater flexibility and efficiency in the deployment of police resources. This option, known as the flexible response model, enhances deterrence and improves passenger perceptions of security by allowing random, uniformed patrol over a wider variety of areas. When using the flexible method of deployment, the

Table 5-1. Criminal Acts Involving U.S. Civil Aviation by Type of Act 1976–1984.

| | | Explosions | |
	Hijacking	Aircraft	Airports
1976	4	2	2
1977	6	1	3
1978	13	0	3
1979	13	1	2
1980	22	1	1
1981	8	0	2
1982	10	1	1
1983	19	0	0
1984	7	0	0

| | Explosive Devices Found | | Bomb Threats | |
	Aircraft	Airports	Aircraft	Airports
1976	1	3	1,950	1,036
1977	2	1	1,229	519
1978	0	6	1,032	318
1979	2	6	1,121	309
1980	1	4	1,179	268
1981	1	6	1,184	400
1982	3	6	887	203
1983	0	1	467	188
1984	1	4	465	139

Source: U.S. Department of Justice, *Sourcebook of Criminal Justice Statistics,* 1985.

airport police administrator must also consider the critical need to strategically place officers around the facility in a means which will enhance the tactical response to a terrorist assault anyplace within the terminal area. Effective police monitoring is necessary throughout all areas of the airport, particularly—as the Rome and Vienna incidents have demonstrated—in the public concourse areas of air terminals.

Formal civil aviation security training for local police assigned to support airline and airport security programs is essential. This training should provide an in-depth background in civil aviation security requirements, procedures and techniques.

Aviation security measures for airlines, airport operators and airport police in the United States are stipulated by the Federal Aviation Administration through Federal Aviation Regulations (FARs). The U.S. civil aviation security program has four components:

**Table 5-2. Criminal Acts Involving U.S. Civil and
Foreign Aviation by Type of Act 1983–1989.**

	HIJACKINGS*		
		United States	
	Foreign	*Actual*	*Prevented***
1983	15	18	7
1984	20	5	1
1985	22	4	4
1986	9	4	1
1987	9	4	0
1988	13	2	1
1989	14	2	0
	BOMB THREATS TO:		
	U.S. Aircraft	*U.S. Airports*	
1983	442	188	
1984	437	139	
1985	477+	153+	
1986	617+	376+	
1987	401	238	
1988	372	256	
1989	479	487	

* includes scheduled air carrier and general aviation aircraft hijackings
** incidents in which it appeared suspects involved intended to hijack an aircraft but were prevented from doing so by security measures
+ This increase may be due in part to extensive publicity related to aviation explosives incidents. See U.S. Department of Transportation, Federal Aviation Administration, *Semiannual Report to Congress on the Effectiveness of the Civil Aviation Security Program, July 1 to December 31, 1988* (Washington, D.C., 1989).
Source: U.S. Department of Justice, *Sourcebook of Criminal Justice Statistics*, 1990.

1. *Air carriers,* who are responsible for the provision of a secure means of transport through the maintenance of responsive security programs, passenger screening, securing of baggage, cargo handling procedures and by protecting aircraft;

2. *Airport operators,* who are responsible for the provision of a secure operating environment through responsive security programs, protection of the air operations (ramp) area, and by providing law enforcement support;

3. *The FAA,* which provides leadership, analysis and the identification of threats, issues security guidelines and requirements (through the FARs), provides coordination and uniformity, and enforces FARs. The FAA also provides technical assistance; and

4. *Passengers* (users), who provide for program costs through a por-

Table 5-3. Results of Airline Passenger Screening, United States 1976-1989.

| | Persons Screened (millions) | Weapons Detected | | Persons Arrested for carriage of Firearms/ Explosives |
		Firearms	Explosive/ Incendiary Devices	
1976	413.6	3,936	8	884
1977	508.8	2,034	5	810
1978	579.7	2,058	3	896
1979	592.5	2,161	3	1,060
1980	585.0	2,022	8	1,031
1981	598.5	2,255	11	1,187
1982	630.2	2,676	1	1,314
1983	709.1	2,784	4	1,282
1984	775.6	2,957	6	1,285
1985	992.9	2,987	12	1,310
1986	1,055.3	3,214	11	1,415
1987	1,095.6	3,252	14	1,581
1988	1,054.9	2,773	11	1,493
1989	1,113.3	2,879	26	1,436

Source: U.S. Department of Justice, *Sourcebook of Criminal Justice Statistics, 1990.*

tion of ticket (user) fees. Users also dictate the level of protection afforded through political action and by influencing market demand.

Effective prevention and mitigation of aviation-directed terrorist assault depends on active communication, cooperation, and coordination among civil authorities, police, emergency service organizations, airport operators and the various airlines. Passenger screening is only one aspect of these needs. Both the tarmac (ramp) area and baggage handling area are vulnerable to assault or bombings. In the past, terrorists have circumvented fixed screening by placing devices and weapons on board aircraft through the ramp area, either posing as airline or airport operations staff, by co-opting staff, or by transferring weapons from one aircraft to another. Increased attention to employee screening and identification/access control is useful in this regard. Passenger-baggage reconciliation is another way to limit the chance of lethal explosive contraband from becoming stored in the hold of the aircraft.

The International Air Transport Association (IATA) has issued an eight-point minimum security standard for airports. These standards, designed to be flexible to ensure optimal cost effective implementation, state that the government or state should provide for:

1. The establishment of a sterile area for boarding all flights. All passengers and hand baggage should be screened before entrance is permitted. Other persons entering this area must be subject to security control and have appropriate authorization.
2. Direct and discrete communications links between screening and access control points should be connected to designated airport control centers with the capability for rapid response.
3. Armed law enforcement officers with communications capability should patrol the airport and be readily available to respond to suspected or actual unlawful acts which interfere with civil aviation. A security crisis management plan must also be in place.
4. Restricted areas must be marked and secured in a way which prevents unauthorized entry of persons or vehicles airside. This access control must be uniformly applied.
5. All personnel airside or in restricted areas must prominently display positive airport identification, which is checked and verified prior to entry.
6. Public areas should be segregated from all baggage and cargo handling areas. Provision should exist to x-ray or screen all baggage and cargo.
7. Aircraft storage areas must be controlled, protected and well lighted.
8. All public areas proximate to the airside must be adequately protected to safeguard security.[9]

It would also be beneficial to provide for airport design which allows open terminals void of places for hiding explosives or storing assault weaponry. The separation of incoming and outgoing passengers may also provide an additional safeguard.

Threat Management

To effectively meet the challenge of terrorism, transportation police need to develop the capacity to systematically process potential terrorist threats. This threat evaluation relies on the development and application of analytic techniques which distinguish between threats which imply an impending risk of serious violence and those which do not.

Transportation managers and the police who protect the transportation facilities need to work cooperatively to develop the scope of response options prior to any incident, and to quickly develop specific action plans based on actual incidents in progress. Accurate and timely collection, recording and evaluation of threat information is essential to an efficient threat management program.

Transport systems benefit from the use of a standardized format for recording threat information. FAA form 1600-53 (a standard bomb threat form) provides an excellent example. These forms should be located at all telephones within the transport facility, particularly at phones in strategic areas such as rail central control facilities, yards, shops and towers; airport control towers and terminal offices; airport crash/fire/rescue stations; public information answer points; and facility police desks. Once received, the information should immediately be relayed to the system's predesignated "decision authority," as well as documented in a transit police report. This information will be used by the decision authority to perform a threat/risk analysis which will guide the development of an incident-specific action plan.

Decision Authority Objectives

The decision authority designates the person(s) responsible for evaluating the threat and making a decision to carry out a specific course of action. The chosen course of action is generally referred to as an incident action plan. Action plans may involve searches, evacuations and the restriction or suspension of service. It is essential that there be only one decision authority for any specific incident. The decision authority may be a single individual—such as a senior police officer of command rank or a senior transportation facility manager—or a joint or "unified" command. A joint or unified command decision authority is usually formed to draw valuable interdisciplinary perspectives into the management of the threat. Typically such a unified command decision authority consists of a senior police official and a senior facility manager who evaluate the threat and develop the objectives for an action plan. Provisions should be made prior to a specific incident for selecting a course of action in case of disagreements among members of a unified structure.

The objectives of a decision authority include:

1. Conducting a threat/risk analysis (i.e., is this specific threat serious—that is, credible and technically possible; what is its potential impact on the transport facility and its patrons, etc.).

2. Determination and communication of incident-specific objectives (i.e., the incident action plan).

3. Determining evacuation parameters. Evacuation parameters vary according to the specific nature of an individual incident, but can be broadly grouped to include: (a) immediate *full* evacuation, (b) immediate *localized* evacuation, (c) personnel work area search, (d) formalized search teams, and (e) specialized searches by bomb squad or explosives specialists, including bomb-detecting dogs.

Threat Evaluation and Risk Analysis

When a threat has been received, it must be evaluated to determine its validity. This process should begin immediately. In addition to validity, the decision authority must also assess the risk to the transport system or facility. Questions which assist in this process include, but are not limited to:

1. When will the act occur? (i.e., when is the bomb going to explode?)
2. Where will the act occur? (i.e., where is the bomb now?)
3. What type of act is threatened? If a bombing is the threat, what does it look like? what kind of bomb is it? what will cause it to explode?

Transport police may benefit from the use of worksheets, which can be developed during a preincident contingency planning process, to facilitate threat evaluation and risk assessment. Worksheets, as analytical tools, can focus the decisionmakers' inquiry, thus ensuring that vital elements of a thorough assessment are not overlooked. During critical incidents, decisionmakers often operate in a chaotic, stress-filled environment and are given large quantities of information to process in a short time. While attempting to sort out this information, decisionmakers are also bombarded by requests from subordinates and peers from affected organizational entities seeking direction or advice. This phenomena— known as becoming overcome by events (or "OBE")—can be managed through the use of incident worksheets and decisionmaking aids.

While each transportation police agency needs to develop its own system specific worksheet, certain common factors need to be considered:

- review threat information
- establish decision authority
- conduct risk evaluation
- determine potential impact
- assess system status
- develop action plan.

Table 5-4. Risk Assessment of Transit System Components.

| Transit Components | Criticality or Level of Impact | | Vulnerability |
	People	System	
Stations	High (a)	(b)	High
Rail			
Track	Low	(b)	High
Cars	High(b)	Low	High
Maintenance yards	Low	Medium	Medium
Switching stations	Low	Medium	Medium
Electric power			
Source for system	Medium	High	Medium
Substations (TPSS)	Low	Medium	Medium
Central control (CCF)	Low(c)	High	Low
Bridges, aerial and tunnel structures	Medium	Medium(b)	Medium
Fans, vents and emergency hatches	Low	Medium	Medium

(a) Depends on what time of day incident occurs: greater impact would be experienced during rush hours than non-rush hours.

(b) Depends on the location in the system where an incident occurs: an incident at a crossover or main junction would have greater impact than one at an outlying station or track segment.

(c) Affects employees only.

Source: Adapted from *Domestic Antiterrorism Efforts at Selected Sites*, GAO/PEMD-88-22

Table 5-4, "Risk Assessments of Transit System Components," was developed by the U.S. Congress, General Accounting Office, and examines the parameters of risk on a typical rail mass transit system using a matrix format. Specific transit components are considered and a qualitative level of risk assigned. Similar risk assessment matrices can be developed for airports, seaports, marine terminals and other transportation infrastructures.

A sample threat management worksheet format is also provided, below, as a model for the development of an agency-specific worksheet.

SAMPLE THREAT MANAGEMENT WORKSHEET

☐ **Review threat information** (e.g., bomb threat card)
☐ **Establish decision authority**
☐ **Conduct risk evaluation**
    ☐ Review "Risk assessment of Transit System Components"
    ☐ Time until threatened act? _____
    ☐ Does the device/act threaten densely populated high volume area?
                                                YES / NO
    ☐ Does the device/act threaten critical resources?
    ☐ Any reason to suggest a hoax?   YES / NO

☐ Is the threatened act feasible or technically possible? YES / NO
☐ Could this be a diversion? YES / NO
☐ Is this threat similar to previous threats directed against this system?
  YES / NO
☐ **Determine potential impact**
  What is the potential impact of the act to:
  ☐ Resources/system HIGH RISK / LOW RISK
  ☐ People/PAX HIGH RISK / LOW RISK
☐ **System status**
  ☐ Normal service
  ☐ Restrict service (localized)
  ☐ Suspend service (systemwide)
☐ **Develop action plan**
  ☐ Implement incident management organization
  ☐ Make appropriate notifications

A thorough and formalized threat evaluation and risk analysis needs to be conducted each time an agency or facility receives a threat. Senior management must communicate and reinforce its commitment to a high quality threat management program to all individual managers and command rank police officers. Many systems receive frequent threats which do not result in actual incidents. This experience may cause some transit personnel to view a new threat as simply more of the same. The lack of prior events can skew the outlook of decisionmakers, potentially causing inattention to a true and present threat. Only if *all* threats are evaluated can an accurate pattern of threat activity be detected.

Ongoing Evaluation of Terrorist Threats

The security of transportation facilities, their patrons and employees is enhanced by the capacity to systematically address a potentially large volume of threats through the application of analytical techniques that distinguish between threats which pose serious risks of impending violence and those which do not.

In an individual threat, the decision authority and an individual command level officer take the first critical steps in threat evaluation and resource allocation. Long-term threat management, however, requires the ability to manage and analyze threat information involving many incidents. This long-term management is essential and requires the assignment of specialized personnel. An agency's detective bureau, in conjunction with specialized external technical specialists, generally takes the responsibility for long-term analysis of threats directed against a specific transport system.

The stages of long-term assessment and analysis include:

1. Evaluation of plausibility on the basis of internal evidence;
2. Verification of information concerning targets, organizations and persons involved;
3. Checks to determine the feasibility of any threatened act of violence;
4. Comparison with similar threat communications received in the past; and
5. Consultation with departmental and extra-departmental experts as necessary.

Response to Actual Incidents

When an agency determines that a particular threat is valid and a response by its field duty force is required, a specific command officer should be designated to direct all incident-related operations. This command officer is frequently known as the Incident Commander (IC) and is responsible for managing the incident and the incident management organization. In all cases, the Incident Manager will have to set incident-specific objectives and an incident action plan for achieving these objectives. Using a bomb threat scenario as an example, we will illustrate an Incident Commander's objectives.

A bomb threat has been received and determined to be valid. The Incident Commander's objectives are to:

1. Size-up (assess the situation);
2. Define objectives and formulate an action plan;
3. Maintain unity and clarity of command;
4. Determine search parameters (search team composition, span of control, systematic and coordinated search patterns);
5. Determine evacuation parameters;
6. Ensure safe search operations (appoint a safety officer, conduct search safety briefings for all incident response personnel); and
7. Keep track of *all* personnel assigned to the incident and all persons who enter the incident ground.

When activating a bomb search operation, the IC may opt to adopt a formalized incident management structure or incident command system as a management tool. When response or search personnel from multiple agencies or disciplines are involved, a unified command structure may be preferred. In order to ensure safe search operations, it is recommended that—regardless of response structure—a safety officer be designated. The safety officer is responsible for briefing *all* response personnel regardless of agency, discipline or function, of *all* pertinent safety issues and safe search practices. General search operations guidelines should be communicated to all response personnel. In many cases the IC may find it desirable to place direct search activities under the direction of a specific person. This person, who may be known as a search branch leader, directs the activities of all search teams. This breakdown allows for a manageable span of control.

Using this format, search guidelines can be summarized as:

1. Never use more searchers than necessary;
2. Always activate a safety officer and consider activation of a search branch leader;
3. Each individual search team should have its own team leader, and search teams should have a minimum of two members;
4. One searcher should search from ground to waist first, then from waist to eye level, and then from eye level to the ceiling. When this is completed, he or she should reverse roles with his or her partner(s).
5. Searches *must* be systematic. Areas searched and then subsequently cleared should be clearly marked;
6. If a suspicious device or article is found: quickly and safely withdraw all searchers to a staging area outside of the inner perimeter and restrict access to all persons. Specialized explosives technicians will then assume any further search operations, device control and management.

When conducting bomb search operations, the following safety objectives must be followed. All transportation system personnel should be familiar with these safety objectives prior to any specific incident and this knowledge should be reinforced prior to response to any specific incident:

1. *No* radios or cellular telephones are to be used in affected areas;
2. Safe search practices are essential;
3. All incident responders need to be advised of safety concerns;
4. Do not touch during search (visual search only);
5. Safely isolate and deny access to area if a bomb or suspicious package or device is found;
6. Clear, isolate and label areas that have been searched and no bomb has been found; and

7. Maintain an awareness of operational concerns and secondary impacts upon the system.

Contingency Planning

Detailed contingency plans are necessary to ensure smooth operations during the critical situations produced by terrorism and acts of extraordinary violence. Plans for incident response should be multilevel, deriving input from all levels of government which will be called into action. Plans should be as close to day-to-day operations as possible and should be frequently reviewed, tested through drills, and updated as necessary. Plans should be flexible and provide the capability for upgrading response. Responsibility should be clearly delineated. Clarity of functional and organizational roles must be maintained, and open communications and ongoing consultation among all personnel should be ensured.

Contingency plans must include, at the minimum:

1. Provision for intelligence gathering and evaluation, including threat and target analysis.
2. Emergency field operations guidelines.
3. A fixed yet flexible incident command structure.
4. The designation of specialized tasks and personnel, including protocols for development.
5. Rules governing the conduct of responding personnel.
6. Rules on weapons use, selection and deployment.
7. Guidelines for negotiations.
8. Provisions for the establishment of a perimeter and operational zones or sectors, including the maintenance of perimeter integrity.
9. Provision for postincident debriefing, critique and, if necessary, critical incident stress (posttraumatic) debriefing and counseling.
10. Provisions for implementation.

Personnel who may respond to critical incidents such as terrorist assault would benefit from ongoing training and familiarization to ensure effective action. A high degree of interagency cooperation is required at all stages of planning, development, training and response to terrorist incidents. For tactical management of a terrorist incident to be successful, police and other responders must match their tactics to overall objectives and avoid response for the sake of response.

Terrorist activity also creates a special risk for private security personnel and agencies which operate at many transportation facilities. With this in mind, the transportation operator or police agency should consider developing a specialized security liaison with the capability to (1) brief private security personnel on the risks and trends in terrorism, (2) provide special briefings on topics such as bomb detection and threat evaluation, (3) include private security managers in contingency planning and (4) detail the role and tasks of private security personnel in the face of an incident.

Special attention must also be given to integrating emergency medical services (EMS), fire and other rescue personnel into the response to terrorist acts. Terrorist assault has the potential to generate injuries or deaths, making EMS response essential. Of 20 European terrorist incidents we analyzed which occurred between April 1985 and April 1986, 681 casualties (injuries) and 110 mortalities (deaths) resulted. Fifty-eight deaths occurred during police counterassault. There were an average of 34.1 casualties per incident and 5.5 mortalities per incident. Injuries had an incidence six times greater than deaths. Clearly this information demonstrates the need to include a medical response into police contingency plans for such acts. From the same data, we find that 75 percent of these incidents were bombings. Considering the possibility of fire related to bombings, fire service response is also indicated.

The large scale injury which can result from terrorist assault demands special medical capability, such as trauma or burn centers, and may overwhelm many EMS and hospital systems. Contingencies for triage, aeromedical evacuation, high-risk transport, bed management and on-scene medical care must be established. External factors such as traffic congestion may hamper transport to hospitals, necessitating field medical management. Only through interdisciplinary coordination can casualties be effectively treated.

Terrorist incidents also pose unfamiliar risks and challenges to rescue personnel. Secondary devices or snipers may threaten their safety and normal treatment protocols may need to be modified. Only through familiarization and planning will EMS providers be able to cope with these situations. Police agencies should take the lead in integrating other essential emergency services into the overall plans for the management of terrorist incidents.

Conclusion

By increasing their awareness to the risks entailed in terrorist assault, transportation agencies and police can become better able to respond to transportation terrorism. Such response includes both prevention and postincident management. By integrating the measures suggested in this chapter with local exigencies, transportation police can become better prepared to manage the threat of terrorism.

Endnotes

1. U.S. Department of Justice, Federal Bureau of Investigation, *Bomb Summary 1984* (Washington, D.C.: FBI Uniform Crime Reports, U.S. Government Printing Office, 1985).

2. G.R. Villar and M.P. Chapman, "Modern Day Piracy," paper presented at the Nautical Institute Seminar on Piracy at Sea, London, 31 October 1986, as reported by Robert G. Moore in "The Price of Admiralty: Regulatory Responses to the Threat of Maritime Terrorism," *Terrorism, Violence, Insurgency Report* (Vol. 7, No. 1, January 1987).

3. Jeffrey D. Simon, "The Implications of the *Achille Lauro* Hijacking for the Maritime Community," *Terrorism, Violence, Insurgency Report* (Vol. 7, No. 1, January 1987).

4. Brian M. Jenkins, *Future Trends in International Terrorism* (The Rand Corporation, P-7176m, December 1985).

5. Simon, "Implications of the *Achille Lauro* Hijacking."

6. Robert G. Moore, "The Price of Admiralty: Regulatory Response to the Threat of Maritime Terrorism," *Terrorism, Violence, Insurgency Report* (Vol. 7, No. 1, January 1987).

7. Ibid.

8. Federal Aviation Administration, U.S. Department of Transportation, *Semi-annual Report to Congress on the Effectiveness of the Civil Aviation Program* (Washington, D.C.: Federal Aviation Administration, 1982).

9. International Air Transportation Association (Montreal, Canada).

Chapter 6

ILLEGAL DRUGS IN TRANSIT

Most law enforcement agencies confront the impact of illicit drug use and commerce each day. Those responsible for the protection of transportation facilities are not immune; in fact, they may be on the cutting edge of the problem. Drugs are an international business. They are produced, marketed, finished, wholesaled, shipped and transshipped. Like any other commodity, they rely upon the transportation infrastructure to get the goods to market and to the end user. Transportation facilities thus become focal points for the movement of illegal drugs, and police who patrol these facilities play a key role in the enforcement of drug laws and in the interdiction of drugs in transit.

Drugs as Big Business

The international trade in illegal drugs is estimated to be worth up to $300 billion per year, with $50 to $100 billion generated in the United States alone.[1] The total money value is greater than that of the oil trade, second only to the arms trade.[2] In one area in one city—South-Central Los Angeles—rock cocaine is a $5 million plus per week business. Law enforcement officials seized more than $100 million in cash from drug dealers in 1988.

But figures in the drug trade are not limited to its staggering illegal profits. Drug use and the drug business contribute significantly to mortality and morbidity rates around the world. In one study of 169 trauma patients randomly screened at the Albert Einstein Medical Center in Philadelphia, three out of four patients had some drug—illicit or prescription—in their bloodstreams. Nearly one-quarter had two or more drugs present. Over half, 54.4 percent, were under the influence of one particular drug: cocaine. The researchers who conducted this study found that "a significantly greater proportion of the violent crime group had been using cocaine" and, aside from the medical consequences of drug use, much of the trauma which necessitated treatment was "a direct result of the violent nature of the drug trade."[3]

Similarly, a 1988 Los Angeles County Department of Health Services study noted that total drug-related cost to the county in the previous year totalled $1.23 billion. This figure included criminal justice costs, emergency medical costs, costs to victims, lost productivity and wages, and the costs of prevention and treatment. One-third of this cost, approximately $400 million, was cocaine-related. All this, while "the entire UN budget for drug control activities is only equivalent to the value of a suitcase of heroin at Heathrow Airport"[4] and 90 percent of all those seeking drug abuse treatment are turned away for lack of such programs.[5]

From Farm to Market

Which nations are home to major drug producers or house major trafficking operations? Iran is an important route for opium and heroin traffic, along with Afghanistan, Pakistan, Laos and Thailand. Myanmar (formerly known as Burma) is the world's major opium producing nation. Mexico is experiencing an increase in drug production of all types. Coca production is centered in Colombia, which processes and distributes 80 percent of the world's cocaine. Bolivia ranks second in world cocaine production, with its neighbors Peru and Equador engaging in both production and money laundering operations. Mexico, Belize, Jamaica and Colombia are important marijuana producers, as is the United States.

Numerous groups are involved in illegal drug marketing. Colombian cartels such as the Medellin and Cali top the list, along with the Jamaican posses ("Shower," "Dog" and "Spanger"), the Sicilian Mafia and the U.S.-based La Cosa Nostra, and black street gangs ("Crips" and "Bloods").

During the late 1980s, the Bush Administration stated that its drug control strategy was to "disrupt and dismantle the multinational criminal organizations that support the production, transportation and distribution of drugs to the United States and other nations."[6] Yet despite the highly publicized U.S. effort to curb drug supply and demand, along with the efforts of the Colombian government against its own drug traffickers, global production of opium poppies, coca and marijuana continues to rise. In 1989, Colombian production of coca rose from 66,700 acres to 103,700 acres. Global drug abuse is also climbing, as higher yields push drug traffickers to aggressively develop new markets.

Stiff penalties don't seem to work either. For example, even though Iran maintains the death penalty for convicted drug dealers, as many as two million regular heroin users persist.

Despite record drug and assets seizures, the capture, extradition and imprisonment of major traffickers, international cooperation and new antimoney laundering laws, "worldwide narcotics production reached new levels, corruption undermined enforcement efforts, and a number of governments still failed to exhibit a serious commitment to reducing drug production and trafficking" according to a 1990 U.S. State Department report on the global drug situation.

Impact on Transit Facilities

Because of the immense profits realized from the drug trade, drug trafficking groups are better organized and have more resources at their disposal than ever before. Faced with increasing governmental resistance to their activities, narcotics traffickers are more often relying on indirect trafficking routes (or "transshipment"). For example, cocaine from Colombia or Peru is likely to be smuggled via Brazil and Nigeria to reach a final destination in Europe or the United States. What happens when their products reach U.S. shores? Let's examine one state, New Jersey, and one drug, cocaine, as a case in point. According to the New Jersey Commission of Investigation, New Jersey is a "microcosm of a commercial system supporting cocaine distribution."[7] New Jersey has a complex, finely developed network of roads, seaports, airports, bridges and tunnels, a transportation infrastructure which is easily used by drug traffickers to move large quantities of illegal drugs with minimal interference. Simply stated, bus and rail systems, airports and seaports afford traffickers a ready-made distribution network.

Consider only one of New Jersey's many transportation facilities, Port Newark.[8] In 1989, Port Newark was the largest sea container port in the United States, and the fourth largest in the world behind Rotterdam, Hong Kong and Koehsiung (South Korea). In 1988, Port Newark handled approximately 6,000 cargo ships carrying 1.7 million sea containers. In addition, an estimated 200,000 containers entered the port by land, on trains under Customs bond from Tacoma, Washington, and Oakland and Los Angeles, California. Of 5,000 containers which enter Port Newark each day, Customs officials are only able to inspect between 30 to 50 containers. Customs and law enforcement officials report that cocaine constitutes in excess of 90 percent of all drugs seized at Port Newark. In 1988, this amounted to 2,882.6 kilograms of cocaine seized at this facility alone. Because of these quantities, officials in New Jersey consider seaports to be a focal point in the importation and distribution of cocaine.

In addition to seizing cocaine, Customs Service agents have found significant quantities of drug paraphernalia, including vials and plastic bags used to hold cocaine finished into crack. Methods of concealment by drug traffickers are diverse and legendary. Customs inspectors have discovered cocaine concealed in plastic tubing for refrigeration, diesel engines, the walls and ceilings of containers, concentrated fruit juices, the walls of cardboard boxes, flowers, chocolates, and even in plastic bags inside the stomachs of live tropical fish. Methods of concealment are "limited only by the imagination of the trafficker. If they can think of it, they will do it until they get caught and then change their method of importation."[9]

Strategies

Faced with increasingly sophisticated tactics and the violent nature of drug organizations, any potential efforts at solving the drug problem must consider the complexities of the issue. The international scope of illegal drug use and trade has long been recognized by police agencies and policymakers. The first World Ministerial Summit to Reduce Demand for Drugs and to Combat the Cocaine Threat, held in London in April 1990, and the United Nations Convention Against Illicit Traffic in Narcotic Drugs and Psychotropic Substances are examples of multinational cooperation aimed at curbing the drug problem.

One hundred twelve nations attended the Ministerial Summit in London, bridging the north-south divide between producers and consumers of illegal drugs. Attendees were quick to point out that expanding drug use has blurred the distinction between producing and consuming nations. In this light, it is clear that international action is necessary, particularly in regard to demand reduction. A 13-page joint declaration issued by the Summit highlighted this position.

The U.N. Convention Against Illicit Traffic in Narcotic Drugs and Psychotropic Substances would allow signatory nations to freeze and seize proceeds derived from illicit drug traffic, and would make all drug trafficking offenses extraditable. Acting as a quasi-extradition treaty between nations which do not have bilateral extradition agreements, the

Convention also contains provisions for mutual legal assistance regarding the gathering of evidence and allowing nations to serve judicial process, execute search and seizure actions, locate witnesses and assist in other procedural tasks for signatory states. The Convention also called for increased security at international ports and on commercial carriers. Parties to the Convention are tasked with ensuring that carriers take reasonable precautions to prevent the use of their equipment as a mode of drug trafficking. Tactically, the Convention advocates "controlled delivery," that is, international undercover sting operations as a means of combatting drug traffickers.

United States' efforts at controlling the illegal drug problem have varied in scope and effectiveness. Active in the "war on drugs" are 11 departments and 37 federal agencies nominally coordinated by the "drug czar." These agencies range from the Pentagon and the FBI, the Drug Enforcement Administration, U.S. Customs and the Coast Guard to the Secret Service. In Congress, 74 committees and subcommittees have jurisdiction over narcotics matters.

Increased military participation in the war on drugs is often advocated in the United States, yet according to a mathematical model developed by a team of Rand Corporation analysts (reported in *Sealing the Borders: The Effects of Increased Military Participation in Drug Interdiction,* a Rand report by Peter Reuter, Gordon Crawford and Jonathan Cane), a more stringent interdiction policy would cut cocaine consumption by less than 5 percent. This Rand study points out that ton-sized shipments of cocaine arrive in the U.S. within such routine cargo shipments as Brazilian lumber and fruit juice pulp.[10]

General strategies addressing drug enforcement are available to police agencies, among them expressive enforcement, or maximizing the number of all types of narcotics arrests. In practice this often results in a large number of arrests for simple possession or being under the influence. Expressive enforcement often has its greatest impact on the urban poor, many of whom are minorities, and has the effect of alienating minority citizens from the police, resulting in increased mistrust and heightened tensions.

Emphasis on disabling high-level distributors is a strategy employed by many police agencies. With this strategy police try to impair the top levels of the drug distribution system by using sophisticated procedures such as wire taps, informants and undercover activities. Gang suppression is another tactic which has gained in popularity since the emergence of street gangs as organized drug traffickers. Street gangs such as Los Angeles's Crips and Bloods are increasingly viewed as organized criminal enterprises with a national scope, and organized crime suppression tactics including electronic surveillance, undercover operations and the use of special statutes such as RICO and similar conspiracy and criminal enterprise legislation are called into play.

Citywide street-level drug enforcement is perhaps the most widely used strategy. Relying on buy/bust operations and the observation of sales, this strategy has mixed results. While often succeeding in restoring the quality of life in a community and reducing fear, it is extremely vulnerable to various forms of corruption.

Neighborhood-specific crackdowns, such as New York's "Operation Pressure Point," are similar to expressive policing, except they target one specific high drug-use area. While they initially reduce street level dealing in the affected areas, drug activity tends to be displaced to other nearby neighborhoods, and the large number of arrests can place a severe strain on other elements of the criminal justice system.

Targeting dangerous offenders is another possible tactic. Police focus on crime control rather than drug control, selectively targeting dealers using violent methods or users engaging in crime to support their habits.

Gaining in popularity, drug prevention directed at children is another law enforcement strategy. Programs such as the Los Angeles Police Department's DARE (Drug Abuse Resistance Education) or the Los Angeles Sheriff's Department's SANE (Substance Abuse Narcotics Education) send police officers into neighborhood schools as teachers. Hoping to educate young people before they become involved in drug or gang activities, these programs have shown much early success.

Clearly no police agency can rely on only one strategy to cope with the complexity of our nation's drug problem. Some of the measures discussed above could be custom mixed to suit the patterns of drug abuse and drug-related crime facing a given community.

Despite the increasing success of enforcement efforts resulting in the apprehension and imprisonment of illicit drug merchants—ranging from the international trafficker to the common street level drug dealer—there has been little indication that such efforts have any significant impact on the price or availability of illegal drugs. Recent U.S. drug strategy has had a supply side emphasis. Yet many if not most drug dealers are not price sensitive. This is particularly true of drug addicts.

When supply is reduced, prices rise—enhancing the profit margin for traffickers while users continue to consume. Another flaw of the supply side emphasis is found in its application. "Although the U.S. is among the top three producers of marijuana, as well as the world's largest consumer of legal and illegal drugs, U.S. policy focuses largely on drugs produced outside our borders."[11] And while more than one-fifth of the federal drug control budget has been used for interdiction, only 18 percent of the drugs smuggled into the U.S. are detected, according to the U.S. Customs Service, not nearly enough to have an appreciable long-term effect on the price or availability of such drugs.

Community Policing

Drug abuse is unavoidably a poverty issue. Only 12 percent of those using illicit drugs are black, but 44 percent of those arrested for simple possession and 57 percent of those arrested for sales are black.[12] Drug usage reflects the many stresses and flaws of American life, and the disenfranchisement felt by many of the urban poor. "The widening gap between the very rich and the very poor in this society can intensify the many frustrations of poverty. In such a heavily materialistic society as ours, both drug use and drug sales can appear to be relatively attractive options."[13]

The impact of drugs on the urban poor as well as other communities across the nation combined with the known criminogenic properties of drug abuse has caused many commentators to look towards community policing as a strategy to cope with drug abuse issues. Patrick V. Murphy, the respected former president of the Police Foundation and Commissioner of the New York Police Department, has observed that "the failures of present enforcement policies make decriminalization tempting. But what we really need is enough eyes in the community and cops on the beat to regain control of our neighborhoods."[14] Murphy notes that enhanced enforcement has not resulted in a reduction of the drug trade. In fact, highly publicized seizures appear to have little or no impact on the availability of drugs on the streets. While the number of persons arrested for drug offenses has been increasing, Murphy points out that "police chiefs in Washington and New York conceded that the arrests benefitted their departments' public image more than they cut into drug dealing." This reliance on police as professional crimefighters may well have limited the effectiveness of a broad-based community response to the drug crisis.

Operations such as New York's widely touted antistreet-level drug dealing "Operation Pressure Point" or the Los Angeles Police Department's antigang "Operation Hammer" rely extensively on police overtime and preempt other police activities. "Citizens, no doubt misled by all the 'film at 11,' may even believe that these operations represent a solid return for their tax dollars," Murphy notes. "But since the supply of police officers cannot keep pace with the public clamor for drug arrests, taxpayers are receiving less overall protection." Murphy states that although legalization may seem an attractive way to cope with the problems of the drug crisis, "experience suggests a better alternative: preventive policing."

Endorsing the growing trend in the police profession towards community policing, Murphy asserts that the police can best facilitate drug control by actively assisting community groups in the exercise of social control. Reflecting the basic premise of the community or neighborhood policing movement, Murphy points out that the community—parents, relatives, friends, neighbors, teachers, clergy, employers—is the primary crimefighting force since it determines the values that make a neighborhood into a community. Police agencies can serve as catalysts for community action.

Mark H. Moore and Mark A.R. Kleiman, prominent scholars and observers of law enforcement, also champion community participation. When dealing with drug abuse and sales, they observe, "the task of a police department is often to find a way to prime the communities' own capacities for self-defense so that police efforts may be effectively leveraged through community self-help."[15]

Moore and Kleiman have identified the goals of police action against drug trafficking and use as:

1. Reducing drug-related gang violence combined with preventing the emergence of powerful criminal organizations;
2. Controlling street crimes committed by drug users;
3. Improving the health, economic and social well-being of drug users;
4. Restoring urban civility and the quality of urban life;
5. Preventing experimental drug use by children; and
6. Protecting the institutional integrity of the criminal justice system.

Conclusion

Whatever the drug enforcement policies adopted on a national or local level, transportation police play an important role in contributing to the chosen policies' ultimate success. Drugs move through our global transportation infrastructure at an unprecedented level. Police agencies at seaports, airports and on rail and highway systems have the ability to offer a wide range of resources to the fight against drug-related crime. Transportation police executives should participate in policymaking decisions at all levels—local, regional, national and international. Transportation police agencies can make significant contributions to and benefit from interagency task or strike forces dealing with illegal drugs.

Transit police also have a vested interest in nurturing the concept of community policing. First, transportation facilities are communities in and of themselves. Commuters, public workers, small businesses and transit police officers form a viable neighborhood each day, and can benefit from community policing techniques and approach. Transportation facilities also form a vital and interdependent part of their surrounding communities. Transportation police executives should encourage their agencies to involve the communities which use and operate their facilities, as well as those which adjoin them, to cooperate in the fight against drug trafficking in their facility.

Endnotes

1. Friends Committee on National Legislation, "The Challenge of the Drug Crisis: To Heal A Wounded Nation," *Washington Newsletter* (February 1990).

2. Ibid.

3. G.A. Lindenbaum *et al*, "Patterns of Alcohol and Drug Use in an Urban Trauma Center: the Increasing Role of Cocaine Abuse," *Journal of Trauma* (29:1654–1658, 1969).

4. Margaret Instree, Coordinator of U.N. Drug-Related Programs, as quoted in Friends Committee on National Legislation *Washington Newsletter*.

5. Source: National Institute of Drug Abuse, as quoted in Friends Committee on National Legislation *Washington Newsletter*.

6. New York *Times*, 2 March 1990.

7. State of New Jersey Commission of Investigation, *Cocaine* (March 1989).

8. Ibid.

9. State of New Jersey *Cocaine*.

10. See also "Can the Borders Be Sealed?" a summary of the Rand report which appeared in *The Public Interest* (Summer 1988).

11. Friends Committee on National Legislation, *Washington Newsletter.*

12. Source: National Institute of Drug Abuse, as quoted in Friends Committee on National Legislation *Washington Newsletter.*

13. Friends Committee on National Legislation, *Washington Newsletter.*

14. All quotes from Patrick V. Murphy from "Drugs: Preventive Policing, Film at 11, But Not Much Protection" in the Los Angeles *Times* (13 March 1990).

15. Mark H. Moore and Mark A.R. Kleiman, "The Police and Drugs," *Perspectives on Policing* (National Institute of Justice, U.S. Department of Justice and John F. Kennedy School of Government, Harvard University, Number 11).

Chapter 7

HAZARDOUS CARGO IN TRANSIT

The transportation of hazardous cargo poses policy, planning, enforcement and response concerns for the transportation police administrator and the specialized police agencies which protect transportation facilities. This chapter will examine the questions which arise from the risks of transporting hazardous radiological and chemical agents, including public safety issues, regulatory statutes, and planning and response to hazardous material accidents for police and other emergency services. Two related topics will also be discussed—the threat of chemical, biological or nuclear terrorism directed against transportation facilities or shipments of hazardous materials, and the controversial issue of police preparedness for potential nuclear accidents.

Hazardous materials, frequently referred to as "hazmat," are those agents which pose a substantial risk to human health or the environment. The chemical industry alone produces more than 35,000 hazardous agents, but hazardous materials may also come from biological or nuclear sources. The Department of Transportation has designated 8,200 hazardous materials, 45 of which may require evacuation or isolation of an area affected by an accidental release.

The potential for serious problems is great. Each year more than several billion tons of hazardous materials are transported throughout the United States in more than 180 million separate movements. Hazardous materials are primarily associated with toxic chemicals such as chlorine or anhydrous ammonia, but chemicals are only one of many toxic agents. Others include biological products, fuel and petroleum products (gasoline is, in fact, the most common hazardous material), explosives, industrial wastes, and nuclear or radiological materials such as spent fuel from nuclear power stations.[1] Nuclear agents alone account for 77,000 cubic meters of material containing 500,000 curies of radiation.[2] This hazardous cargo is transported in approximately 500,000 daily air, sea and land shipments. Motor-truck shipments comprise around half of this activity, with 80 million tons shipped by rail yearly and 610 tons by ship or barge.[3] Hazardous materials incidents from all forms of transportation yielded 24 deaths, 663 injuries, and property damage amounting to more than $13 million between 1973 and 1983.[4]

A Los Angeles *Times* analysis[5] of 67,702 hazardous materials incidents reported to the U.S. Department of Transportation between 1982 and 1991 showed that hazardous materials incidents, nationwide, rose 37 percent during that period. During this ten-year period, rail incidents increased 36 percent and incidents involving motor carriers increased 34 percent. Of the 67,702 incidents analyzed by the newspaper, 81.4 percent involved motor carriers (trucks on highways); 14.6 percent were rail-related; 2.4 percent involved air carriers; and 1.6 percent occurred at other locations. These incidents resulted in 108 deaths (highway 98.2 percent; rail 0.9 percent; other 0.9 percent); 2,827 injuries, and 25,513 evacuations. Motor carriers accounted for the largest proportion of injuries, with 70.9 percent of the injuries occurring on the nation's highways. Rail incidents followed, with 19 percent of the injuries. Aviation incidents made up 6.7 percent of the injuries, and 3.4 percent occurred at other locations. In the 25,513 incidents resulting in evacuation, rail incidents accounted for 61.2 percent; highway incidents 37.1 percent; and incidents at other locations 1.1 percent of the total. Despite these high figures, the U.S. General Accounting Office has estimated that only 11 to 20 percent of all hazmat incidents are actually reported.[6]

In many areas the potential effects of incidents are heightened by the possibility of synergetic effects resulting from a multiple agent incident. This could happen, for example, when two separate hazardous materials carriers are involved in one incident. "The confluence of hazardous material and nuclear waste transportation routes increases the probability of a severe accident involving both types of substances. Examination of 1,100 hazardous materials accidents reported to DOT [the U.S. Department of Transportation] between 1977 and 1981 shows that 40 percent of these accidents took place along designated nuclear routes."[7]

While the probability of a hazmat incident involving a toxic chemical or radiation release cannot be predicted, accidents can be prevented and their impacts reduced. Enforcement, regulation and training play a key role in prevention, and improved emergency response capability (including planning and training efforts) can minimize deleterious impact.

Enforcement

All levels of government—federal, state and local—are intimately involved in ensuring the safe transport of dangerous cargo, in preventing accidents which may lead to hazmat scenarios, and in containing the release of toxic substances. The federal government has the primary role and takes the lead by issuing regulations, classifying materials, and specifying labeling and placarding of hazardous shipments. State agencies are involved in inspection and enforcement. Local government, particularly police and fire departments and emergency medical services (EMS), ensure and provide frontline emergency response. Municipalities also attempt to prevent potential incidents from occurring through enforcement efforts and imposing restrictions on routes and times of transport. Forty-six states, 127 localities and 28 transportation agencies or authorities have rules and regulations regarding the transportation of hazardous or radioactive materials.

Federal regulation, enforcement and emergency response for hazardous materials is divided among 12 federal agencies or bureaus. Within DOT, seven separate agencies handle distinct aspects of hazmat regulation. These agencies are the Office of Hazardous Materials Transportation, the Federal Highway Administration, the Bureau of Motor Carrier Safety, the National Highway Traffic Safety Administration, the Federal Railroad Administration, the Federal Aviation Administration, and the U.S. Coast Guard. The Office of Hazardous Materials Transportation, the Federal Highway Administration, the Federal Railroad Administration, the Federal Aviation Administration and the Coast Guard have inspection and enforcement responsibilities. The Coast Guard also has emergency response duties. Three independent regulatory agencies—the Environmental Protection Agency, the Nuclear Regulatory Committee and the Department of Energy—have both enforcement and emergency response duties.

State authority for handling hazardous materials is generally divided among a variety of agencies. The state police or highway patrol usually conducts inspections on public roadways, while a separate agency is involved in terminal inspections. Common problems identified by state enforcement agencies include inadequately displayed placards, improperly identified hazardous wastes, and the lack of or inadequate shipping papers.[8]

A Virginia Department of Transportation study found that at least one-third of all trucks hauling hazardous cargo were improperly labeled.[9] This is particularly alarming since the identification of hazardous shipments by placards and shipping papers provides valuable safety information to first responders to hazardous cargo dispersal incidents.

The enforcement of hazardous materials violations differs from state to state, and also within states. Violation rates are impacted by enforcement policies. When violation rates are low, this may not indicate that fewer instances of improper hazardous cargo handling occurred. Rather, it may mean that unequal enforcement methods were used. Some states or localities issue only warnings, and others provide only for civil actions. In the states with the most stringent regulations, hazardous materials infractions are treated as misdemeanors.

Consistent state enforcement policies are necessary, especially when local prosecutorial agencies and courts unfamiliar with the risks involved underestimate the serious nature of hazardous materials violations. The U.S. Congress Office of Technology Assessment reports that enforcement agents have identified four commonly experienced difficulties in the prosecution of hazardous materials violations. Cases must be set aside or charges reduced when officers do not gather enough documentation in their inspection reports, or when they do not follow procedures correctly. It also happens that judges unfamiliar with hazardous materials regulations respond to enforcement efforts by dismissing cases or lowering penalties because of the difficulties they encounter in understanding the regulations. Enforcement officials also have trouble securing assistance from other agencies in the preparation of evidence, and feel that fines are too low, so that they do not serve as a deterrent to noncompliance.[10]

Specialized training, knowledge, skill and experience are necessary if enforcement officers are to adequately inspect vehicles carrying hazardous cargo and accurately identify breaches of federal and state hazardous materials regulations. A state enforcement training program which may serve as a model for developing the necessary skills for these tasks is currently run by the California Highway Patrol (CHP). In their program, CHP inspection officers spend twenty weeks in a basic hazardous materials inspection procedure training course. Officers then go to the field under supervision of veteran CHP inspectors, where they receive an additional thirty days of training. Throughout the year refresher training courses are offered, and officers must return to the academy every three years for in-service training. Officers who serve at inspection and scale units receive an additional 80 hours training in commercial enforcement and must retrain every two years. They are selected for duty from the ranks of veteran inspectors.[11]

Local government agencies are primarily involved with emergency response to hazmat incidents. In many cases local government may also have enacted supplemental prevention-oriented regulations such as restricting the routes and hours of hazardous cargo shipments, enacting requirements for advance notification and escorts, and requiring special permits or licenses.

Hazardous cargo travels not only on land but by water and air. Hazmat incidents at marine transportation terminals or adjacent ports and harbors are a potential concern of marine or port authority police agencies. This is particularly true since the tonnage of hazardous materials transported via vessel and barge appears to be growing. Larger ship size, greater vessel speeds and denser marine traffic increase the likelihood of marine accidents as well. Since some of the larger tanker ships measure their turning and stopping distances in miles rather than yards, action must be taken long in advance to avoid collisions. Barges also have mobility problems.

Air transportation of hazardous cargo is also filled with potential risks. Hazardous materials sent by air are regulated by the FAA through Federal Aviation Regulations (FARs) and, as such, are subject to enforcement by the FAA's Civil Security Division. In addition, local airport authorities may have their own requirements for supplemental information. Newark International Airport (Newark, New Jersey) and John F. Kennedy International Airport and LaGuardia Airport (both located in New York), for example, have notification requirements for the shipment of spent nuclear fuels and other radioactive materials, as well as for other hazardous materials.

Response

Emergency response to hazardous materials incidents is another area where the police of a transportation agency or facility may be involved. Any accident where cargo is unidentified, and vehicles have improper or no placards, is a potential hazardous materials incident. Comprehensive preincident contingency planning is essential for the successful management of a toxic accident. Preincident planning should anticipate, and on-scene response/management requires, a high level of interagency coordination and cooperation. Often the police will take a lead in pre-incident planning and in many cases will coordinate and direct on-scene incident management. Effective management of a toxic incident will demand cooperation and coordination. Cooperation and coordination require a thorough integration of police activities with the activities of the fire service, rescue personnel, EMS and often local hospitals and burn centers.

The train accident and ensuing fire at Rockingham, North Carolina in March 1977[12] pointed out the consequences of a lack of coordination among emergency responders and the need for comprehensive preincident planning. The Rockingham accident involved both hazardous radiological (uranium hexafluoride) and chemical (ammonium nitrate) materials. The incident began as a train derailment and rapidly accelerated. Upon impact, four containers of uranium hexafluoride were scattered, and a car carrying ammonium nitrate caught on fire. Shortly after the accident occurred, the train crew notified the railroad dispatcher. The railroad had no emergency response plan or notification procedure in place, but the dispatcher alerted the organizations which he thought might be helpful. Notification took three hours. The local fire department arrived on the scene thirty-five minutes after the accident. They were the first responders. Five minutes later, local police and the state highway patrol came to the scene. Three hours later the highway patrol attempted to determine if radiation was leaking from the accident site, but none was detected. Shortly after this attempt, a U.S. Army Explosive Ordinance Disposal team arrived and believed that radiation was in fact leaking. The Army assessment led to a halt in recovery operations. Later that afternoon a Department of Energy team from Oak Ridge National Laboratories came to the site and conclusively determined that radiation was not leaking. In all, eighteen separate organizations responded to the incident yet no one agency assumed control. All agencies conducted their tasks on an individual basis. This lack of leadership and coordination also led to confusion concerning technical aspects of response—no one was sure how to extinguish a fire involving uranium hexafluoride, and several conflicting approaches were suggested.

Interestingly, at least ten separate existing emergency response plans could have been applied to the incident. None of these plans, however, was comprehensive or addressed coordination with the other plans. Additionally, none of these plans designated an incident command structure or provided a definition of the roles of the agencies involved, or delegated functional responsibility. The state and local agencies assumed that the Department of Energy (Energy Research and Development Administration team from Oak Ridge) would take charge because of their expertise, but the team did not believe it could assume control from the state. The presence of more than one hazardous material and the lack of coordination complicated response to this incident. If a comprehensive written preincident plan envisioning a variety of events had been developed, field management of this incident could have proceeded smoothly, unencumbered by a lack of clarity and discipline.

Police and firefighters were the first to arrive at the Rockingham incident. No casualties occurred at the accident but if they had, emergency medical service response would have been indicated. Often the local emergency medical service is overlooked in contingency planning and preincident drills, yet the potential medical consequences of hazmat incidents and the potential life threatening nature of exposure to many hazardous and toxic agents make EMS participation essential. Past radiological incidents have shown that local agencies such as police, fire and EMS are usually the first to respond to such accidents. Trained personnel from state agencies typically arrive many hours later.[13] These first responders are often unable to deal with the problems associated with radiological materials. An Indiana State University study found that less than a third of the local police departments in thirty states (out of thirty-five states which returned questionnaires) had any personnel trained in the use of radiological emergency equipment. In three of these states, no local police were familiar with the equipment.[14]

In order to provide adequate response to a hazmat or radiological emergency, preparedness in the following areas is necessary: (1) proper equipment for first responders, (2) training programs for local police, fire and EMS personnel, (3) interagency cooperation, coordination and communication, (4) multiple emergency communications systems on common frequencies and (5) contingency plans. Concerning communications, many areas rely extensively on police radio systems for emergency needs, yet only a few police agencies have common or compatible radio systems or frequencies—a great detriment in the event of an emergency requiring cooperation among agencies.

When developing plans for responding to hazardous materials incidents, it should also be remembered that emergency response to an incident does not "freeze" all other normal or crisis activities. Accordingly, contingency planning should include provisions for sustaining normal activities and allow the capability for response to more than one serious incident at one time. Also, not all incidents will require maximal response. Therefore, all aspects of a given plan may not have to be implemented for every incident. Since a hazardous incident may be dynamic, changing from a low intensity to a high intensity during its course, the capability to upgrade response as necessary needs to be included.

Six major elements common to preincident planning[15] can be described as:

1. Analyzing the most likely sources of accidents and emergencies.
2. Assessing the nature and effects of the chemical(s) likely to be released.
3. Defining the role and activities of the incident commander and command post.
4. Establishing standard operating procedures for handling specific accidents and emergency response.
5. Identifying resources and training personnel.
6. Preparing a systematic method for ongoing incident analysis and the collection, collation, evaluation and reporting of information.

The contingency planning process should be multidisciplinary, drawing resources and information from all levels of government. In addition to various police agencies, the fire service, transportation and port authorities, the public health authority, EMS and the chemical industry and utilities should be represented. Plans need to be reviewed and updated on a frequent basis. Plans also need to be tested in regular drills which will provide the necessary information for fine-tuning response.

Because of the potential hazards to health, toxic and nuclear emergencies can easily result in mass hysteria and panic. Situations which require evacuation are especially likely to trigger these feelings. Because of this possibility and the civil unrest which may follow, civil government must avoid losing control of the situation or the appearance of having lost control. As always, the police have the primary responsibility for the maintenance of order and public safety. This responsibility makes the development of a response to hazmat incidents by the police essential. Police cooperation and coordination with other public safety agencies, particularly the fire service and EMS, is crucial, given the special risks hazmat incidents may pose. Integration of emergency response capability in this manner assures quick, decisive action which helps to minimize fear and disruption of normal activities.

Effective field response to a hazardous cargo incident should include the following four elements.

1. ***Delineation of responsibility.*** This includes designating the lead response agency and incident scene commander, and defining the role of each agency involved along with the role of individual personnel. Fragmented response and interagency rivalry must be avoided. Clarity of organizational role is assured by maintaining open communications and thorough ongoing consultation among those responsible for overall management and those responsible for direct line supervision and operations.

2. ***Scene assessment and agent identification.*** Immediate hazards and the nature and extent of the incident must be determined. The agent should be identified and its properties determined. Response protocols will be determined by the actual agent(s) spilled or released and their properties. If the agent is not readily identifiable, responders must assume the worst case scenario and act accordingly.

3. ***Securing a perimeter/maintaining control of the scene.*** This is one of the main duties of a police agency at a hazmat scene. Access to the immediate scene must be limited to appropriate and essential emergency response personnel. If protective gear is indicated, only appropriate protected response personnel should be allowed access beyond the perimeter. Perimeter integrity must be maintained along with order.

4. ***Designation of zones of operation.*** Operational zones within the perimeter may be necessary. The area within the perimeter is the incident ground. Typical zones include contamination, control (also known as containment) and safe (or safety) zones. These zones generally form concentric circles or eclipses around the immediate incident site with the contamination zone closest to the immediate scene (or site of spillage), and the safe zone closest to the perimeter. The activities which occur in each zone may differ according to incident type but should be anticipated for various hazmat scenarios. The protocols for intrazone activity should be clearly stipulated in the preincident contingency planning process.

When an accident involving the dispersal of hazardous chemical, biological or nuclear materials occurs, governmental and police response is necessary. Generally, incident response will follow the pattern detailed below.

Once discovered, the police and/or other appropriate government authorities are notified. The police usually receive first notification. Upon notification, the appropriate police and emergency response personnel are dispatched. Police crowd control units, scene containment and perimeter maintenance units are included as are hazmat teams (personnel with special training for handling such incidents), the fire service and emergency medical service (ambulance) units.

When the first crews arrive, scene assessment and agent identification occurs. Scene assessment includes an evaluation of the overall nature of the incident as well as a determination of the special needs of each emergency service (i.e., more police units to handle crowd situations, additional ambulances and EMS personnel when multiple casualties are suspected, specialized fire apparatus, cranes for moving large trucks or railway cars). After assessment, appropriate assistance will be requested.

If the toxic material is not yet identified or its properties are not known, assistance for identification may be indicated. Chemtrec, the Pesticide Hotline or the Centers for Disease Control may be resources for this need. After agent identification, rescue begins.

The rescue phase has two distinct components, human and environmental. Human rescue includes victim (casualty) extrication; evacuation of threatened population areas; treatment for life-threatening injuries; decontamination; triage; and transportation to an appropriate medical facility. Environmental rescue involves the decontamination of vehicles, gear and equipment, and the clean-up of the affected area.

Special Circumstances: CBN Terrorism

Similar to hazardous materials incidents are possible terrorist acts employing chemical, biological or nuclear (CBN) agents. These incidents are alike since both are environmental emergencies with potentially catastrophic effects. Acts of CBN terrorism and hazmat incidents both involve "a hostile environment requiring containment, specialized response and management; the potential for multiple casualties; and risk to emergency response personnel."[16] In both types of occurrences, police response to the hazards posed is essentially the same. In the intentional terrorist-orchestrated hazardous materials incident, however, law enforcement protocols for response to an investigation of terrorist incidents would also come into play. Although a cursory examination of either CBN terrorism or conventional hazmat incidents may lead police administrators and policymakers to assume that these occurrences are vastly different, a closer examination shows that both phenomena have many common elements. Developing a response capability for hazardous materials incidents allows for control and remediation of CBN terrorist incidents as well. Response capabilities are piggybacked in a way that provides efficient response capability without the duplication of valuable resources.

While terrorists are unlikely in the near future to embrace the destructive capabilities provided by chemical, biological or nuclear technologies since current tactics and weaponry provide the desired effect, consideration of this possibility cannot be avoided. For a variety of reasons ranging from the continued effectiveness of current terrorist modes—including aircraft hijackings, bombings, assaults with conventional weapons, kidnappings and assassinations—to an avoidance of supra-violent tactics which could endanger popular support and political "legitimacy," terrorists have for the most part refrained from using CBN modalities. Many terrorist groups do not have the organizational stability, sophistication and internal specialization which are required to utilize advanced technologies. Dispersal devices for CBN agents are complex and difficult to build. The fabrication of devices which could deliver CBN agents in an effective manner requires highly technical skills. Nuclear agents are difficult to obtain and the construction of a nuclear explosive device, contrary to popular belief, is a technically demanding task. Chemicals, on the other hand, are easy to obtain but delivery presents many difficulties.

Despite terrorists' reluctance to use CBN methodologies and the difficulties encountered in their use, the risk remains. "Urban areas with their concentrations of communications centers, bridges, tunnels, transportation terminals and office buildings are potential targets for CBN attacks. Subway systems and office buildings are especially vulnerable to application of aerosol agents because of their closed nature. Shipments of hazardous agents—chemical, biological or nuclear—would also be a prime target for terrorist appropriation or attack. A terrorist operation against a shipment of CBN agents or hazardous materials could be a hijacking in order to appropriate the materials or a more conventional attack aimed at extortion or release of the agents."[17]

If current terrorist methods begin to prove ineffective, terrorist groups may become attracted to new and innovative technologies. High levels of violence and more lethal attacks have been the traditional terrorist response to improved counterterrorist strategy by governments. As government better coordinates its response to terrorism and hardens potential targets, terrorists may counter by including CBN tactics in their attack repertoire.

Additionally, the acts of fanatical groups or individuals driven by political or ideological motivations cannot be discounted. Therefore, police agencies need to consider the threat of planned intentional hazardous materials incidents—CBN terrorism. Responding to CBN terrorism requires the same skills, equipment and planning which are required to handle unplanned, accidental hazmat incidents.

The threat of a terrorist-instigated hazmat incident is currently not great. Conventional hazmat incidents are many times more likely to occur. The multiplicity of toxic agents which are shipped across the nation as hazardous cargo make the risk of accidental release a genuine threat, however, which requires careful planning. Including the risk of CBN terrorist attack into this planning is a prudent act in the face of the current world political climate.

Ethical Issues: Police Preparedness for Nuclear Accidents

The diversity of issues arising from hazardous materials and the impact these issues can have on policing decisions is highlighted by the controversy surrounding emergency planning at nuclear power stations. Although these are not primarily transportation-related issues, they underscore the complex ethical questions involved in the police handling of hazmat incidents. Transportation police would possibly participate in evacuation efforts at these sites and may be called in to provide mutual aid. Controversy is centered around the participation of local police and emergency services in planning for "extraordinary nuclear occurrences" at the Shoreham reactor in Suffolk County, New York, and the Seabrook reactor in New Hampshire.

Local and state government and police agencies have refused to cooperate in the development of emergency plans for these reactors, stating that no conceivable emergency plan could work in an actual emergency. This refusal to become involved in the contingency planning process is a highly political decision since the plants are not yet in full operation. In the case of Shoreham, state and local officials contend that the plant's site—on the north shore of Long Island, 55 miles from New York City—makes an effective evacuation in the face of a nuclear accident impossible. These officials point out that moving a large number of people over already severely congested roads would be folly, particularly when people would be in a state of near panic. They also point out that since Long Island can only be exited in one direction, west, those persons in affected areas to the east of the plant would be forced to pass through the most dangerous areas to complete an evacuation. Similarly, state and local authorities in Massachusetts have refused to join in the evacuation planning process for the Seabrook nuclear plant located two miles across the New Hampshire border.

Federal regulations require a 10-mile evacuation zone around all nuclear reactor sites. By opting not to cooperate in the planning process, state and local officials have kept these plants from going into operation.

Advocates of nuclear power have called local police and governmental agencies irresponsible for not participating in planning efforts and have asserted that they are interfering with commercial activities. Despite criticism, the government, police and emergency services agencies have refused to yield. At Shoreham, the Long Island Lighting Company (Lilco) which operates the plant has tried to circumvent the actions of the state and municipality by developing an evacuation plan on its own. Lilco, in an attempt to meet the federal requirements, drafted its own emergency evacuation plan substituting meter readers, linemen and other utility workers in the place of police officers and other government officials. These Lilco proxies were to direct traffic and coordinate the evacuation of Suffolk County on their own. Suffolk County, however, challenged Lilco's evacuation plan in court, asserting that the utility was attempting to usurp a legitimate function and power of the state. The assertion of the municipality was upheld by a New York State appeals court.[18] The court ruled that Lilco does not have the legal authority or standing to carry out its own emergency evacuation plan. The court noted that if Lilco were to implement its plan, its action "would result in a usurpation of the state's police power" and that this power resides exclusively "with the State and its duly authorized political subdivisions." Providing protection for people and property "is at the core of the State and local governments' police power," the court emphasized.

This controversy led to heightened public awareness of the issue. In the case of Shoreham, the utility opted to cancel the project. Shoreham is now closed and is currently being dismantled, never having gone on line. No doubt the controversy is not over. Power plant operators still maintain that plants should go on line with or without local participation in planning for accidents. Also, the Nuclear Regulatory Commission (NRC), in an attempt to override local objections to the licensing of reactors, has drafted a proposal which would allow the commission to waive its requirements for emergency planning and a 10-mile evacuation zone. The reasoning behind this waiver is the assertion that if an emergency were to occur, police and emergency services would have to respond regardless of the existence of emergency plans. Of course, this is true. In any emergency the police and civil authorities will respond. But experience has shown that response is not what matters; rather, it is the quality of the response. In a situation involving hazardous chemical, biological or nuclear agents, preincident planning is especially important. Given the highly lethal nature of these agents, panic, fear and mass hysteria are possible. Only with well-thought-out, clearly defined emergency plans will civil government be able to maintain order.

No police official wishes to endanger the public. Yet in the case study presented above, several police administrators and officials of civil government and other emergency services have opted not to be involved in the generation of emergency plans as a matter of conscience and as a deliberate effort to influence public policy. These officials have decided that their action (or nonaction) is just and avoids the development of a false sense of security among the populace. The relative merits of their decision will no doubt be debated in the courts and by the electorate. Only public sentiment, the judiciary, and ultimately the experience of time will render a final decision. Yet the case as presented above illustrates the depth of a seemingly mundane police function—emergency planning.

In this controversy the discretionary power of the police as a government agency and the police administrator as a policymaker is brought to light. As community concern heightens over the siting of not only power stations but chemical plants, hazardous waste dumps, and other potentially dangerous complexes, it becomes increasingly clear that this discretionary power will have large consequences and that ethical decisions will more often weigh on the mind of the police administrator.

These questions are not only for the general service police. When transported, hazardous materials are hazardous cargo. Even the Shoreham plant will generate spent fuel which must be transported to a reprocessing plant—by truck, by rail, by barge, over the highways, across bridges and through tunnels, off-loaded and on-loaded at marine terminals, rail terminals, and motor truck terminals. As this material is transported, the transportation police administrator is faced with the same ethical issues which were confronted by the local police in Suffolk County. Even if this issue does not arise in a transportation context, the specialized transportation police as part of the overall police network will be called upon for aid and assistance in evacuation plans and contingency measures for civil emergencies.

Endnotes

1. Office of Technology Assessment, *Transportation of Hazardous Materials: State and Local Activities* (Washington, D.C.: U.S. Government Printing Office, 1986).

2. Taylor Moore, "The Great State of Uncertainty in Low-Level Waste Disposal" in *The Electric Power Research Institute Journal* (March 1985) as reported in the Office of Technology Assessment's *Transportation of Hazardous Materials: State and Local Activities.*

3. Office of Technology Assessment, *Transportation of Hazardous Materials.*

4. Ibid.

5. "America's Poisons on the Move," Los Angeles *Times* (20 September 1992).

6. Marvin Resnikoff, *The Next Nuclear Gamble: Transportation and Storage of Nuclear Waste* (New York: Council on Economic Priorities, 1983).

7. Ibid.

8. Office of Technology Assessment, *Transportation of Hazardous Materials.*

9. J.W. Schmidt and D.L. Price, *Hazardous Materials Transportation in Virginia* (Richmond, VA: Department of Transportation Safety, Commonwealth of Virginia, 1980).

10. Office of Technology Assessment, *Transportation of Hazardous Materials.*

11. Ibid.

12. Office of Technology Assessment, *Transportation of Hazardous Materials.*

13. Nuclear Regulatory Commission, *Social Impacts of the Transport of Radioactive Materials in Urban Areas* (Washington, D.C.: September 1980).

14. Nuclear Regulatory Commission, *Survey of Current State Radiological Emergency Response Capabilities for Transportation-Related Incidents* (Washington, D.C.: September 1980).

15. These elements identified by the World Health Organization International Program on Chemical Safety were reported by F. Pocchiari and V. Silvano in "Coping with Accidents and Emergencies Involving the Release of Potentially Toxic Chemicals" in *Emergency and Disaster Medicine,* C. Manni and S.I. Magalini, eds. (Berlin: Springer-Verlag, 1985).

16. John P. Sullivan and Peter C. Caram, "Planning the Police Response to Chemical, Biological or Nuclear Terrorism and Hazardous Materials Incidents," *Terrorism, Violence, Insurgency Report* (Volume 7, Number 1, January 1987).

17. Ibid.

18. This unanimous decision of a four-judge panel was heard in the Appellate Division of the New York State Supreme Court. The decision handed down by Justices William C. Thompson, Richard A. Brown, Geraldine T. Eiber and Joseph J. Kunzeman was reported in the New York *Times* (10 February 1987).

Chapter 8

PUBLIC BUS/RAIL TERMINAL CRIME

Public bus and rail terminals are an important component of many transportation systems. Surface transit in the form of buses frequently forms the backbone of many regional transport systems throughout North America and, indeed, throughout the world. Many travellers rely upon buses for occasional long distance journeys or more frequent local and regional trips. Generally buses fall into three classes: (1) intercity or long-haul carriers; (2) regional commuter/express services which provide frequent, limited service to the region's central business district and (3) urban or local service.

Many commuters rely upon regional or urban surface transit buses for transportation to and from work, school and vital services such as shopping or medical care. A comprehensive framework for ensuring safe and secure terminals and surface transit is a necessity for transit operators and police—both specialized transit police and general service police agencies.

Transportation Terminals

Like railways, intercity and regional commuter or express bus services often operate to and from major terminals. These bus and rail terminals share many characteristics, among them the problems of crime and disorder.

Modern public bus and rail terminals—such as New York City's Port Authority Bus Terminal, San Francisco's Transbay Terminal, Jersey City's Journal Square Transportation Center, along with their older rail counterparts such as Grand Central and Pennsylvania Station in New York and Los Angeles' Union Station—are intermodal transportation centers which are frequently viewed as economically productive property independent of their transportation functions. Such terminals serve as community gateways and civic centers, often forming the anchor for urban renaissance movements.

These modern terminals operate and are managed in a highly integrated fashion. Typically, they attempt to offer a first-quality transport hub in conjunction with a competitive retail environment. These modern centers rarely rely on any one transport mode. Rather, they seek to operate as multimodal loci for transfer among modes along with access to a variety of convenience, financial and cultural services. Such a mix may include taxi-bus-rail combinations, and often involves access to multiple forms of rail or bus transport. These combinations attract large numbers of diverse people to the facility. The diverse nature of terminal users along with potential high crowd density provide unique challenges to the police responsible for maintaining the public peace.

Consider just one major rail terminal, New York's Grand Central Station. On a typical weekday 150,000 passengers traverse its corridors, waiting rooms and concourses. They utilize ticketing areas and information services, and seek gate access to subway trains, 550 daily Metro-North commuter trains and 60 weekly Amtrak trains. Specialized retail stores and restaurants benefit from this activity, forming an economically productive tenant base for the terminal operator.

Unfortunately, this activity and the central location of many transportation terminals also have the potential to make these vital facilities a loci for crime and disorder. The police who protect these facilities face theft, pickpocketing, fraud, bunco and con games, vice activity such as prostitution, drug use and sales, passenger assaults and robberies. Quasi-criminal disorder problems such as loitering, runaways, truants and groups of homeless persons congregating in public areas exacerbate the impact of criminal activity in terminals. (The problems associated with homeless persons in transportation facilities is discussed in depth in Chapter 9.)

Crime in the Terminals

While passenger assaults and robberies are perhaps the most dramatic of criminal problems faced by police in a terminal environment, they generally do not occur with great frequency. Their serious nature and resulting impact on patron willingness to use a particular facility are of paramount concern, however. Techniques for the management of these incidents are widely understood throughout the police service and typically involve suppression through high uniform patrol, plainclothes anticrime or decoy operations, and crime prevention activities.

Theft, such as the theft of unattended baggage, is a problem specific to this environment and is also addressed through similar means. Disorder-related issues such as panhandling, which frequently borders on theft through intimidation (known as "panhassling"), loitering and vice activities are harder to counter and, as a consequence, can significantly impact patron levels of fear. In some terminals, a growing number of persons loitering in the facility are engaged in drug sales necessitating an increased transit police role in street-level narcotics enforcement. Since this typically involves new skills for transit officers, increased interaction with general service police agencies should be considered.

Pickpocketing is a problem which all terminal police must be able to recognize and counter. Large numbers of people gathered in a compressed space make transportation terminals an attractive site for pickpockets to work. Travellers distracted by high activity levels, concerns about making connections, in a possibly unfamiliar territory, and handling money for ticket purchases give pickpockets an advantage. Trained observers of human activity and experts in distraction, pickpockets are often highly skilled "artisans." They employ a number of techniques to steal wallets, jewelry or money, often working in a crowd to minimize the risk of detection and to widen the choice of potential victims.

Pickpockets may work alone or in organized groups of two to five persons. Generally, the pickpocket leads the group. Known as the "pick," "dip," or "hook," the pickpocket will manually remove the victim's property. The "stall" maneuvers the victim into a position of advantage for the pickpocket and the "tail" remains to the rear of the group, where he or she may receive the wallet and remove its contents. Pickpockets usually use an object such as a coat draped over an arm, a newspaper or magazine as camouflage. After removing the wallet, it is often concealed in this hiding place. If the theft is discovered, the covering object is discretely discarded, allowing the pickpocket to elude detection.

There are many techniques in use by pickpockets around the world, and often a pickpocket will acquire a particular specialty. The techniques are known by a variety of names, depending upon location, but a pickpocket's procedure generally involves victim selection; maneuvering the victim into position; the removal of the target wallet or object; transfer of the object to a secondary group member; and the getaway.

Countering and catching pickpockets is a specialized and demanding police activity. Transit police agencies faced with pickpocket activity may find that the establishment of a specialized pickpocket detail is a beneficial response. Prior to deployment, members of the detail would benefit from time spent working with an established airport, transit or municipal police pickpocket squad. Team members must be familiar with the *modus operandi* of pickpockets who operate in their area. They must also have patience, superior skills of observation, and must be able to blend unobtrusively into their surroundings. They should be aware of unusual actions such as a person following another for a long period of time, a person looking into women's purses, a person who circles a crowd or spends inappropriate amounts of time around ticketing or gate areas, a person who enters and exits ticket or waiting lines repeatedly, or persons who periodically get together and then separate. Antipickpocket officers generally work in plainclothes to avoid shifting activity to areas without uniformed patrol presence, but uniformed officers should have an awareness of pickpocket tactics as well. Additionally, uniformed officers can be used in conjunction with plainclothes teams during specialized pickpocket suppression and detection operations.

There are many scams, con games, bunco and fraud activities which present a concern for the police at transport terminals. These activities defraud transit patrons, contribute to perceived and actual disorder, and foster patron distrust of transit in general. Many of these activities such as card games—three card monte, for example—which involve theft by trick or deception are seemingly minor issues to many patrons yet are intimately tied to other terminal disorder issues. Other fraud activities are difficult to detect and many victims are reluctant to report their existence to police due to embarrassment. Terminal police need to actively protect patrons from these activities by engaging in patron education programs and high visibility interaction with all terminal users.

One recent scam of growing concern in transportation terminals throughout the United States involves phone cards. The growth of the public's use of long distance calling cards has provided a new venue for criminal activity. In these scams, the perpetrator obtains telephone calling card personal identification numbers (PINs) by observing legitimate callers in the process of dialing a number. The perpetrator then sells the PIN to others or approaches persons making long distance calls and offers to make the connection for them at a reduced rate—which he or she pockets. The phone call is then charged to the unsuspecting initial caller. Many unsuspecting travellers as well as telephone services are thus victimized. Terminal police need to be aware of this practice and should monitor phone banks to detect this fraudulent activity. Additionally, travellers should be educated about the risk and be advised of security measures. Transit police countering this problem need to work closely with telephone company security personnel and prosecutorial authorities in order to achieve success.

Since many transport terminals are in the downtown area of major cities, runaways from around the nation and truants from within a region are drawn to them as focal points for activity. These runaways and truants often become victimized and drawn into a wide variety of vice and narcotic-related crimes. Transportation police in several cities have found that specialized efforts to assist these juveniles can improve patron perceptions of security, reduce disorder on connecting transit systems, and minimize the effects of victimization by returning the juveniles to their home or school.

An early and successful example of a terminal police juvenile intervention effort is found in the Port Authority of New York and New Jersey's Youth Services Unit. Established in 1976, the unit is based at the Port Authority Bus Terminal in New York's Times Square/42nd Street area—notable, unfortunately, for its high levels of prostitution and illegal drug activity. The unit utilizes police-social worker teams who patrol the bus terminal with the goal of engaging juveniles who congregate in the terminal to provide skilled intervention. The Youth Services Unit provides crisis intervention linking at-risk youth with supporting services, counseling and, in many cases, the reuniting of runaways with their families. This pioneer team demonstrated the potential for successful joint police-social services efforts and in many respects acted as a forerunner to modern community-oriented, problem-solving efforts in policing.

Policing the Terminals

Providing a secure and safe environment for the customers, tenants and employees who use public rail and bus terminals is vital given the important role these facilities play in any region's transportation network. Transport terminals, like transit systems in general, are part of the greater community at large and also function as communities in and of themselves. Because of this dynamic position, the police who work in transit facilities must come together with these communities—both internal and external—to develop customized programs, strategies and objectives. Police administrators and command level staff responsible for guiding terminal policing activities must recognize the need to channel the goals and objectives of the community, the patrol force and the police department itself into a cohesive effort that maximizes all aspects of a customer's experience with the transport terminal. By necessity, this goes beyond the traditional view of police activity. Many issues of significant stature in the transit environment, as well as in the community at large, are not amenable to enforcement-only responses. Modern police, particularly those who police transit systems and transport terminals, need to broaden their perspective to include actions which draw upon the combined strength of joint problem resolution, community advocacy and order maintenance.

Police assigned to transport terminals must be sensitive to transportation customer/patron concerns. Key among the activities which address customer/patron concerns is maintaining a sense of order. This can be facilitated through high visibility officer activities that emphasize frequent police-public interaction. High quality police-public interaction involves many activities: active enforcement of quality-of-life violations; providing referrals to appropriate external community services; actively providing crime prevention advice to travellers, commuters, tenants such as shopkeepers, and transit employees; and seeking customer input into problem identification and the development of strategies to address them.

Another method of ensuring high quality interaction is the deployment of patron assistance kiosks. These kiosks are self-contained substations which can be positioned at highly visible locations within a transport terminal. The kiosks can serve as focal points for public contact activities such as providing travel information, taking reports, and providing assistance. When not staffed, a patron assistance phone would be made available. Kiosks have been successfully used by a number of police agencies around the world, including those in Hong Kong, Singapore, Japan, Brazil and South Korea.

Surface Transit, Crime and Disorder

Crime, disorder and their impact on public mass transportation—both rail and surface (bus)—have remained an issue of paramount concern to transit patrons and operators over the past several decades. Potential transit patrons often decide to use or not use public transit based upon their perception of safety. While riding on a transit vehicle, passengers often perceive that their personal mobility is limited. Due in part to this impact of perceived security on patron choice regarding transit mode as well as structural elements of the transit environment, transit security has become an important element of any community crime control strategy. Transit security, likewise, has become an integral component of most transit operations.

In many respects surface transit crime is similar to its rail transit counterpart. Key issues which have been identified on urban or regional bus systems include passenger and driver assaults and robberies; fare evasion; the production, use and sale of counterfeit fare media; vandalism, particularly graffiti; employee theft and fraud; street gang activity; and quality-of-life or disorder issues. Intercity buses generally don't face these problems on a large scale, but some evidence exists that these bus services are increasingly being used by drug traffickers as part of regional and national narcotics distribution conduits.

Specific strategies and tactics for policing buses are not covered here since in many ways they mirror those employed on rail systems. Despite the similarities, however, distinct differences exist in the policing of buses. With notable exceptions in Los Angeles, Houston, Atlanta and Washington, D.C., surface transit systems are usually policed by local police jurisdictions rather than by specialized transit police. Consequently, there is no accurate, separate accounting of crime and disorder on board buses or at bus stops. Despite this lack of data and a reluctance by transit operators to acknowledge problems if they exist, bus patrons appear to share the same concerns as their rail counterparts.

Transit crime—particularly bus-related transit crime—is an issue which concerns the entire community and, as such, deserves a central role in any community crime control strategy. Transit police must actively involve community members—bus riders, local police, residents and merchants who live or work adjacent to transit lines—to take a role in protecting and ensuring the viability of the system.

Transit police need to go beyond their traditional system-specific bias and seek the support and advice of external sources. They need to serve as a catalyst, within the transit system, for greater involvement of the public in such decisions as route placement, bus stop and terminal location and design, and service operating hours and practices. This broadened perspective necessarily includes the need for closer coordination and cooperation with local providers of police service. Transit police need to meet regularly with their local counterparts at all levels of each organization to forge interdependent community-based problem-solving activities. This collaboration should draw from the strengths of both types of police organizations, with the health and wellbeing of both the transit and general communities as their overall guides to decisionmaking.

A first step in forming this essential collaboration could be the development of transit familiarization training for local police. Many regions served by buses, particularly those with major bus terminals, would benefit from the development of a standard surface transit training program for all peace officers/police agencies within their service area. Such a program could include practical seminars to familiarize police officers with the impact of bus-related transit crime upon the quality of life within the communities they serve. These seminars could familiarize local general service police officers with the transit-specific sections of the applicable penal or criminal codes within their region. This type of training could also familiarize police with techniques for patrolling and monitoring the buses which traverse their patrol areas, and contribute to a broader understanding of standardized, safe techniques for managing high risk incidents on board buses. Additional areas which could be addressed include familiarization with such problems as graffiti vandalism and tagging, as well as methods for ensuring ongoing liaison and cooperation between transit police and their general service counterparts.

Common training combined with increased interaction with local police providers, transit operators and transit police can contribute to management of transit crime and disorder issues in a way that enhances the quality of community life. Such programs can benefit local police agencies and their officers by enhancing their knowledge and skills related to transit crime incidents.

Conclusion

Crime and disorder at public rail and bus terminals and on surface transit buses are issues of concern to the transit community. Public bus and rail terminals in major cities with established transport infrastructures often benefit from coverage by experienced specialized police agencies or units. As public transit, particularly rail transit, becomes more prevalent, the need for this special expertise within both specialized and general service police agencies can be expected to grow in importance.

The nature and extent of criminal activity and disorder on urban and regional bus lines is less clear and deserves increased research and scrutiny. Active efforts toward defining the scope of these issues on surface transit are needed. A uniform definition of transit crime as related to buses must be developed, and statistical data needs to be routinely collected and analyzed.

Finally, police programs for bus and rail terminals as well as surface transit systems must integrate the needs of their communities—both internal and external—as they continue to evolve into high quality mechanisms for ensuring the public peace.

Chapter 9

SPECIAL PROBLEMS IN
URBAN TRANSPORTATION CENTERS:
THE HOMELESS AND THE MENTALLY ILL

Homelessness is one of America's most pressing and sensitive problems, and perhaps the one most difficult to resolve. Men, women and families, for a variety of reasons, find themselves unable to enjoy the security of a roof over their heads, forcing them to seek refuge in parks, abandoned cars and buildings and the streets. Despite the national scope of this problem, the homeless are most evident in our nation's cities. *Time* magazine has estimated that there are more than 350,000 homeless nationwide.[1] Of this number there are approximately 25,000 homeless persons in Chicago,[2] 20,000 in Los Angeles,[3] and as many as 60,000 in New York.[4] The actual numbers may indeed be higher. Many urban homeless seek shelter in bus stations, train and ferry terminals, subways and other transportation facilities. It has been estimated that 750 to 1,000 people live in transportation centers in the New York metropolitan region alone.[5]

There is no "quick fix" for homelessness. As Philip W. Brickner *et al.*, in the preface to their book *Health Care of Homeless People* noted:

> Our country and its people are now suffering the onerous consequences of earlier social policy decisions. Among these are real estate practices in major urban areas that have allowed low-cost housing to shrivel or disappear; economic planning that has led to structural unemployment, especially among young minority group people; and the enforced deinstitutionalization from state hospitals of the chronically mentally ill. Thousands of these individuals are now helpless in the streets of our cities.
>
> Total solutions to these complex problems are not evident today. We have, instead, an opportunity to work together in tangible ways.[6]

The homeless and the concurrent problem of the mentally ill pose many difficulties for the agencies which operate and the police who patrol urban transportation centers. This chapter will attempt to outline some of the tangible means of addressing these problems as manifested in transportation facilities.

The Problems

Transportation centers are not intended to be shelters for homeless and disaffiliated persons. Rather, they provide a central point for transfer from one form of transport to another. These terminals also provide snack shops, newsstands, information counters and other services for commuters and long-distance travellers. The presence of homeless persons often compromises and disrupts the normal functioning of a facility.

Not the least of the problems is the aesthetic quality of the environment. Homeless people dressed in rags, filthy clothes or plastic bags lying on a floor littered with cardboard boxes and old newspapers—often smeared with urine or feces—are not an appealing sight. Homeless persons bathing in sinks, living in water closets or sleeping on benches take the problem a step further by interfering with the travelling public's use of these facilities. Homeless people wandering around in various stages of undress, engaging in sexual relations in open view, muttering obscenities or panhandling in a menacing fashion offend the sensibilities of travellers and make them feel threatened. Intoxicated or emotionally disturbed homeless persons engaged in bizarre conduct, screaming matches or fights further disrupt normal activity. Social order is perceived to have broken down and, once the perception of societal decay and a "poor police presence" take hold, a deviant fringe group which preys on the homeless is invariably attracted.

The homeless on the streets pose problems for police and social service providers but, as evidenced above, a concentration of alcoholic and mentally ill homeless in one specific place creates special difficulties. Not only does the presence of the homeless place stress on the facility's operation by compromising its intended use but it also results in a lower level of safety and an accompanying increased demand for police service for both criminal and noncriminal matters.

Rather than blaming the homeless for their condition and the problems which face police and transportation operators, it should be noted that the problems experienced by transportation centers are minuscule when compared to the day-to-day ordeal of the homeless person. Clearly a transportation center is not the appropriate place for anyone to live. Waiting room chairs, stairwells and cold floors are no substitute for warm beds. Despite the presence of a uniformed patrol force, the homeless who congregate in transportation centers are frequently and repeatedly robbed of the few possessions they have, are assaulted and even occasionally murdered. Female and young male homeless persons are also frequent victims of sexual assault and rape. Although no figures are available for crimes committed solely in transportation centers, female homeless are victims of these crimes with a frequency many times greater than in the general population. In a startling example, 9 percent of the assault victims treated by San Francisco's Sexual Trauma Service were homeless — an incidence greater than 20 times the occurrence among the general population. One-half of these *reported* assaults resulted in injury.[7]

Homeless people in transportation centers are often the victims of insensitive treatment by passersby and police who are frustrated by the seeming intractibility of the problem. In many cases these homeless are denied access to human services such as social services and medical and psychiatric care because of the lack of coordination in the human services system.

Homelessness is not a crime. Rather, it is a condition and a social — not a police — problem. However, police involvement in this problem is essential and unavoidable. In the past, homeless persons who congregated in transportation centers were treated as vagrants or loiterers. As society became more aware of homelessness as a condition and of civil rights and liberties in general, the courts in various jurisdictions decriminalized these activities.[8] Many police agencies and transportation operators also decided as a matter of policy not to evict homeless persons onto the streets. As a result, police generally no longer evict, summons or arrest homeless persons who seek refuge in transportation facilities. Yet, because of the criminal activities which have come to be associated with areas where the homeless congregate, police become involved.

The presence of homeless persons poses a uniquely frustrating challenge for police who maintain order in transportation centers. Police officers play a dynamic and critical role in the operation of these facilities by aiding travellers, seeking to deter crime by patrol and "community" liaison functions, and intervening in crisis situations. Since they are often the only available representatives of government, they have a responsibility to protect and aid the homeless. In fact, the police represent an essential point in the handling and referral of homeless persons.

Because of this, without effective police procedures, outreach programs and other services for the homeless can only be marginally effective.

Homeless persons commonly experience a variety of health care problems including alcohol and drug abuse; respiratory diseases; infestations such as scabies and lice; ulcerations of the skin; trauma; seizure disorders and emotional and psychiatric problems.[9] Since the homeless—particularly those who congregate in transportation facilities—are often unable to negotiate their own health care, their disorders lead to a request for police assistance. Police become the only access point to health and psychiatric services for many homeless people, resulting in an increased demand for noncriminal police response (known as aided cases). The diverse nature of the homeless population means that there is no simple solution or group of services available to aid all members of the group.

Many of the persons who congregate in transportation centers have been homeless for a long period of time and are known by the officers who police the centers. Those who have explored shelter programs and other services often return to the facility, and a large percentage of the homeless are resistant to using shelters or other services of any kind. In both cases the homeless people prefer the familiar environment, resources and anonymity provided by the transportation center. This resistance to service programs is usually the result of generalized fear or mistrust, attributable to previous bad experiences or prior inappropriate or inadequate referrals, but it may also result from a perception on the homeless person's part that acceptance of service will yield a loss of independence.

An article in the *Journal of Police Science and Administration* has suggested that "handling the mentally ill is the single most perplexing type of call most law enforcement officers are asked to handle."[10] Since many homeless who gather in transportation centers suffer from some form of mental illness (and alcoholism), 80–90 percent in the current authors' experience, it is not surprising that most police officers prefer to avoid interaction with the homeless.

Yet the homeless are not the only mentally ill persons police officers face in transportation centers. All situations where the police confront mentally ill or emotionally disturbed persons require special care. Police dealings with the emotionally disturbed entail a risk to both the responding police, the disturbed individuals themselves, and the public. Between 1974 and 1983, twenty-three police officers were killed in such incidents.

In 1983 alone, 1,089 law enforcement officers were assaulted by emotionally disturbed persons.[11]

A study by Abt Associates, a Cambridge, Massachusetts consulting firm, reviews the interaction between police and the social services regarding the homeless, the mentally ill, and public inebriates. Funded by the National Institute of Justice, the study found that serious problems arose for law enforcement officers who dealt with these populations. The report cited frustration, stress and loss of time which could have been devoted to other essential police duties as major concerns for the officers. These factors often result in a feeling of ineffectiveness for the individual officer, coupled with a general loss of morale. They may also damage an officer's confidence in his or her superiors.

The Abt study noted that officers' frustration was particularly acute when their own feelings of stress, resulting from their inability to help those in great need, were added to the public's demand for them to handle the problem. The stress was further complicated by the officers' perception that, in dealing with the homeless, they were engaging in an activity which they were not adequately trained to handle and which they did not have the responsibility to solve. Few police officers can avoid being sympathetic to the homeless and their plight. When faced with homeless persons' resistance to aid combined with an often unresponsive human services system, however, morale is diminished even among the most dedicated officers.

Roots of the Problem

Mental illness and homelessness are sensitive issues which frequently overlap. Deinstitutionalization has played a role in each. Deinstitutionalization was based on legal and philosophical concepts which were intended to protect individual liberty. Advocates of the concept were convinced that institutionalization in a state hospital did not treat mental illness but deprived individuals of the liberty to freely move about and participate in society. Advocates felt that once free from imposed "incarceration" in large mental hospitals, individuals would choose, in their own best interests, to accept community-based treatment. Unfortunately, this was not the case. Community-based treatment for the mentally ill was never fully implemented because of lack of funding and public resistance to the placement of services in their neighborhoods, among other reasons. Once let out onto the street, often with inadequate prerelease planning for postinstitutional case management, many deinstitutionalized persons were left with no alternative but to seek shelter in transportation facilities and other public spaces.

Ironically, the policy of deinstitutionalization, which was intended to further the exercise of liberty, has interacted with other social and economic forces to preclude the exercise of freedom. It gave homeless persons the liberty to languish in the streets and transportation facilities of the nation—untreated and thus without the capacity to enjoy their rights or any meaningful freedom.

A vivid example of deinstitutionalization can be seen in the case of "Al," a long-term habitue of a major urban transportation center. Smoking cigarette after cigarette, Al would pace up and down the concourse area of the facility each day. Police officers repeatedly tried to engage him in conversation, asking him if he would like to go to a shelter. Al refused to speak to the officers or to anyone else. He kept walking around the facility, pausing only to urinate on the walls or occasionally to masturbate in a corner. This activity eventually led to his arrest. After a few days in a county correctional facility, Al was released and he returned to the transportation center. This pattern was repeated over a period of two years before Al started to become physically ill.

Luckily for Al, a social worker became interested in him. Making a real effort to break down Al's resistance to talk, he succeeded in discovering his full name. Armed with this information, the social worker was able to check Social Security disability and Medicaid rolls. The social worker found that Al had a history of schizophrenia and had spent many years in a state hospital. He had been deinstitutionalized from the asylum of the hospital into the care of his sister. He had only lived with his sister for about one month, however, before she, too, was hospitalized for schizophrenia. With no place to stay and no access to his medication, Al drifted into the transportation center and remained there. In this case and many others similar to it, the post-deinstitutionalization, community-based, psychiatric/mental health care system failed. Fortunately, Al's story turned out better than most. Finding that he was entitled to benefits, Al was able to be placed in a sheltered boarding-home arrangement where he had access to medical and psychiatric care. It is a sad fact that many other homeless persons residing in transportation facilities have not found such satisfactory living accommodations.

Steps Towards Solutions

For police, transportation operators and human services providers to better address the problem of homelessness in transportation facilities, the distinction between the homeless who gather there and the homeless population in general must be recognized. Confusing these populations has resulted in human service programs that have often failed to assist those who reside in transportation centers. Traditionally, shelter and housing opportunities were believed to be the remedy to the homeless problem, yet the homeless who choose to live in transportation facilities have been particularly resistant to such service. When they have utilized shelters, the result has been less than satisfactory in many cases. Shelters alone cannot meet the needs of all the transportation center's population. The more adaptable—or well—among the population go to the shelter and accept service. However, the more severely disaffiliated either leave the shelter by choice or violate shelter rules and are evicted. In both instances, they return to the transportation facility, many times bringing new acquaintances back with them. This experience demonstrates the need to design and implement population-specific human services which gear their service package to the target population.

Many transportation agencies have developed outreach efforts to attract homeless from transportation centers to use available services. These efforts range from providing police officers with a list of referrals and guidelines for response to the homeless to more sophisticated outreach teams composed of police, civilians or a combination of the two. This type of outreach team is intended to encourage homeless persons to voluntarily seek shelter or related services, but its effectiveness is often limited by a lack of specialized training. Without this training, an important ingredient is missing—a fully developed linkage to a comprehensive range of human services.

To bridge the gap between safe facilities for the public and the management of individuals who seek refuge there, viable linkages between police and human service agencies must be forged. Linkages with social service and mental health resources in the community can prove to be an effective way of solving the problems encountered by police. Further, formal linkages minimize the chance of inappropriate police referrals which can cause problems for human service agencies.

Effective linkage relieves police officers from handling individuals with noncriminal psychiatric, medical or economic problems, and also benefits human service providers by ensuring that police refer these individuals to agencies with trained staff who can aid or treat the individuals' problems. An effective linkage effort for handling the homeless and mentally ill will integrate the ability to screen individuals for the appropriate referral, identify available and appropriate facilities and services for referrals, and provide on-scene crisis intervention on a 24-hour basis.

Linkage can be accomplished by outreach efforts such as medical-psychiatric assessment teams. These teams can be staffed by specially trained police officers or by social workers hired by the transportation agency or by police and social workers from a third agency who act individually or under contract to the transportation agency. No matter what their source, the medical-psychiatric assessment teams must work closely with facility operations staff, the police who patrol the center, and other human service providers.

Police participation in assessment teams often helps to save police time, reduces danger to officers, the public and the disturbed individual involved, and increases morale and job satisfaction. The Los Angeles Police Department, for example, "determined that social workers operating out of four police substations reduced the threat of danger in 15 out of 63 cases they were called to handle, as well as saving police time in 19 cases."[12] Social workers familiar with the population are often able to impart valuable information to police officers responding to a situation involving the homeless or the mentally ill person, such as the knowledge that a particular person has a history of violent behavior. The Abt Associates study mentioned earlier states that job satisfaction and morale are improved because there are fewer repeat cases, more appropriate dispositions are made, and thus the image of the police is enhanced. Human services agencies also benefit since inappropriate referrals area avoided and intake processing and evaluation are streamlined.

A liaison person (either a civilian or a sworn officer) acting as a "Homeless Coordinator" or "Social Services Coordinator" may prove to be another valuable addition. This person could help coordinate response to the problem of homelessness and also monitor the success record of various programs. Mutual crosstraining for police and outreach social workers is also important. Each discipline could provide familiarization sessions for the other, enabling barriers to be broken which result from personal or professional mistrust and bias. Training will help promote cooperation by giving human services workers an inside view of the situations faced by police officers, and by giving police officers the chance to develop diagnostic and crisis intervention skills.

By bringing assessment and treatment to the facility, medical-psychiatric assessment teams can enable professional monitoring and intervention of chronically homeless persons who would otherwise be unwilling to be seen and treated. The teams could "monitor individuals who refuse treatment and involuntarily commit those individuals who are immediate risks to themselves and others."[13] Special psychiatric crisis teams composed of trained mental health workers might be an additional aid. Assisting police in emergent crisis situations on a 24-hour basis, these teams could be piggybacked onto medical-psychiatric assessment teams to provide on-scene intervention or general guidance via a telephone hot line. Local exigencies would determine which model best meets local needs.

Involuntary commitment needs to be explored as a means of ensuring that the mentally ill—homeless or otherwise—receive required care. Under current mental health laws, involuntary commitment is difficult to accomplish. In New York state, for example, involuntary psychiatric admission or hospitalization is only allowed if there is a likelihood of serious harm to the mentally ill person or others. Eccentric behavior or choosing to remain homeless in deplorable conditions would not be considered criteria for admission. The American Bar Association has suggested that commitment criteria be expanded to include persons "who appear so gravely disabled as to be unable to provide themselves with the basic necessities of life."

With many possible tools available, the basic techniques of repeated engagement and trust-building will still be the medical-psychiatric assessment team's greatest asset in attempting to persuade the homeless and mentally ill to accept referral to service. Although these teams are a positive step towards resolving the problem of homelessness in transportation facilities, it is unlikely that they will ever be fully successful. The comprehensive range of psychiatric and mental health services which were provided by state hospitals prior to deinstitutionalization are not available to this population, and currently existing services are segmented and parochial. Further, services when provided are often cursory and lack the benefit of a well planned, individually tailored treatment package. To a great extent, this lack of service quality and quantity is the result of an inadequate development of funding for community-based treatment facilities in the wake of deinstitutionalization. The few community-based facilities that have been developed do not have the necessary resources to successfully provide for the needs of the population. How then can police and mental health linkage efforts be proven to be effective? The Abt study noted specific criteria for judging the effectiveness of cooperative efforts, including:

1. The number of cases diverted from the criminal justice system.
2. The number of police hours saved.
3. The number of cases where the threat of danger was reduced.
4. The number and type of police referrals to agencies and facilities.
5. The number of police referrals hospitalized.
6. The number of police referrals who voluntarily accepted treatment.
7. The percentage of appropriate police referrals.
8. The number of times police assisted facilities in handling violent clients.

These criteria could be useful in the ongoing evaluation of programs designed to tackle the problems facing transportation agencies.

Current Working Models

Finally, two interesting models involving police in Los Angeles and sheriffs in Galveston, Texas, are worth noting for their innovative approach to handling mentally ill and homeless persons.

In Los Angeles, public outcry after the death of a police officer at the hands of an emotionally disturbed person prompted the Los Angeles Police Department to develop a more adequate response to handling the mentally ill. A 24-hour police Mental Evaluation Unit (MEU) was designed. When Los Angeles police officers encounter a person with mental health problems, they call the Mental Evaluation Unit to speak with a specially trained MEU officer. The MEU officer prescreens the case, suggesting guidelines for its management, and can provide on-scene assistance or direct the officers in the field to bring the individual to the Unit office. When psychiatric care is indicated by MEU assessment, the patrol officer transports the individual to a hospital where rapid psychiatric evaluation can be conducted. Better police-hospital relations result from the confidence psychiatric residents have developed in MEU referrals.

MEU generally handles over 200 calls monthly,[14] since all Los Angeles Police Department officers are directed to contact the Mental Evaluation Unit whenever screening or transporting suspected emotionally disturbed persons. Before booking a mentally ill person for a criminal offense, MEU contact is still mandated.

MEU officers are trained by a social worker from the Los Angeles Department of Mental Health and receive special instruction from the Los Angeles District Attorney's Psychiatric Section. Preliminary evaluation of the Mental Evaluation Unit's impact on the Los Angeles Police Department shows that police time was saved in 19 out of 63 cases; 18 clients were directed to treatment; threat of danger was reduced in 15 cases; and 10 arrests were prevented.[15]

Large cities such as Los Angeles are not the only areas to create innovative concepts. The Galveston County, Texas, Sheriff's Department developed a specialized unit of five Mental Health Deputies. Although the Sheriff's Department serves an area with a population of only 194,000, the Mental Health Deputies receive six to twelve calls daily from their own and neighboring departments. These specially trained deputies respond to cases involving the homeless, alcoholics and persons with acute drug or alcohol problems requiring detoxification, as well as the mentally ill. The deputies operate out of the local Department of Mental Health and Retardation offices, and have received extensive paraprofessional training. A nine-month Emergency Medical Technician training course is included, followed by an additional nine-month internship with the Department of Mental Health and Retardation where casework, crisis intervention and diagnostic skills are stressed.

These two program models from two widely different general service law enforcement agencies provide insight to policymakers, police administrators and transportation center operators who are striving to deal with the growing problems of the homeless and mentally ill in our nation's transportation centers. The problems are extremely difficult to resolve. Only through thorough analysis, commitment and innovative action can the problems be remediated and the plight of the homeless and mentally ill be made less disheartening.

Endnotes

1. *Time* (2 February 1987).
2. Task Force on Emergency Shelter, *Homeless in Chicago* (Chicago: October 1983).
3. Los Angeles Police Department estimate, 1985.

4. Coalition for the Homeless estimate, as cited in the New York *Times* (14 April 1985).

5. Henry I. DeGeneste and John P. Sullivan, "Urban Transit Centers: Where Crime and the Homeless Meet," *Law Enforcement News* (February 1987).

6. Philip W. Brickner, *et al*, eds., *Health Care of Homeless People* (New York: Springer, 1985).

7. The figures are based on data from John T. Kelly, "Trauma: With the Example of San Francisco's Shelter Programs" in Philip W. Brickner, *et al*, eds., *Health Care of Homeless People* as reported in "Trauma and Exposure Among the Homeless" by John P. Sullivan in *JEMS: The Journal of Emergency Medical Services* (Vol. 11, No. 11, November 1986).

8. DeGeneste and Sullivan, "Urban Transit Centers."

9. John P. Sullivan, "The Homeless: Responsibilities and Guidelines for EMTs and Paramedics," *JEMS: The Journal of Emergency Medical Services* (Vol. 11, No. 11, November 1986).

10. Wayne B. Manewicz, Lynn M. Fransway and Michael W. O'Neill, "Improving the Linkages Between Community Mental Health and the Police," *Journal of Police Science and Administration* (1982, Vol. 10, No. 2) as reported by Abt Associates.

11. Figures from the U.S. Department of Justice, Federal Bureau of Investigation, *Law Enforcement Officers Killed and Assaulted, 1983* (Washington, D.C.: Uniform Crime Reports, U.S. Government Printing Office, 1984).

12. Peter Finn and Monique Sullivan (Abt Associates), *Police Response to Special Populations* (Washington, D.C.: National Institute of Justice, October 1987).

13. DeGeneste and Sullivan, "Urban Transit Centers."

14. Finn and Sullivan, *Police Response.*

15. Ibid.

Chapter 10

CONCLUSION

The secure movement of people, goods and information is essential to the functioning of modern society. Economic, political and social stability depend upon it. Ensuring this free movement are the transportation systems—roadways, passenger and freight rail lines, aircraft, ships and ferries.

Commerce, diplomacy, and the routine tasks of living are carried out in countless journeys each day. Throughout these journeys, the people, goods and transportation mode itself must be secured and protected. Crime and disorder in their many variations are constant threats to this smooth exchange. *Policing Transportation Facilities* has reviewed the major issues concerning the security and policing of these vital conduits with the intention to provide a framework for informed decision making.

The Role of Police

Police responsible for protecting urban transport systems, airports, maritime port facilities and all other forms of goods and passengers in transit play essential roles in ensuring the economic and sociopolitical stability of an increasingly volatile world.

Mounting concerns about crime, violence and environmental catastrophe are a common theme in the public policy arena. These issues clearly have the potential to impact vital transportation infrastructures. An understanding of crime's dynamics and its impact on transportation facilities is therefore necessary. Police and law enforcement authorities both in the community at large and in the specialized environment of the transit center can benefit from this information. While knowledge of specialized transport police issues is key, an understanding of recent developments in policing as a whole is also important.

Community-oriented Policing

Over the past decade, much research and practical effort have been focused towards redefining the parameters of policing. This effort is loosely termed "community" or "problem"-oriented policing. While several definitions of these terms are offered by different observers and theorists of policing, it is generally agreed that the movement involves a shift from an enforcement focused, incident driven model[1] which emphasizes crimefighting (i.e., rapid response and quick return to patrol) to a problem-solving approach, which is intended to bring the police into a closer collaboration with the community they police in an effort to address underlying problems. This shift promises such a wide range of possibilities for improving the response to challenges—including citizen disenchantment, escalating violent crime, increasingly complex and demographically diverse communities—that it has been called "a quiet revolution" by eminent police scholar George Kelling.[2]

As members of the transit police service in the United States have assessed their progress in relation to their general police service counterparts, it has become apparent that problem-solving approaches offer similar benefits when extended to the transit environment.

In "Transit Police and Their Communities," George Kelling and William J. Bratton, then Chief of the New York City Transit Police Department,[3] identified common elements of community/problem-oriented policing, including the focus on problems instead of incidents; the building of police-community partnerships as a means to determine priorities in policing; an integration of the police with other community and neighborhood resources; the transfer of authority to lower levels to facilitate responsiveness to community and neighborhood issues; and, most importantly, the recognition and acceptance of the full range of legitimate police activities including law enforcement, order maintenance, conflict resolution, problem solving and emergency services.

Kelling and Bratton identify three core problems clustered in public transportation facilities: robbery, farebeating (fare evasion or theft of services) and disorderly behavior. While these problems also exist in the general policing environment, they are of paramount concern in the transit setting.

Consider robbery and disorder. While important issues on the streets, they are acute concerns on transit systems since the systems' economic health and continued viability are dependent upon voluntary usage.

Kelling and Bratton observe that the fear attributed to disorder is more acute in the transit setting than on the street since transit users are confined within the system—generally unable to flee at will, thus contributing to enhanced perceptions of helplessness vis-a-vis crime and disorder. Among the fundamental community policing principles which they identify as relevant to transit policing are a focus on problems, preventing crime and, most importantly, order maintenance as an end in itself and as a means of reducing fear and preventing crime.

Along the same lines, Phyllis McDonald, a researcher and administrator with the New York City Transit Police Department, has observed that several differences between urban and transit policing should be recognized during the development of transit policing strategies.[4] The need for a high visibility patrol presence, an integration of nonpolice transit employees into a comprehensive transit crime and disorder strategy, and a recognition of the importance of order maintenance rank high among her list of concerns. McDonald, recognizing the traditional bias towards "crimefighting" and felony crime control, advocates a broad range of police activities, including the acknowledgement of formerly low priority issues such as fare enforcement. She states, "A new definition of 'policing' must evolve which includes disorder and fare evasion and not just felony crimes. Police departments can achieve these results in two ways: by emphasizing order maintenance and by exhibiting strong, highly visible and effective police activity."

McDonald points out that since transportation policing is not driven by calls for service, it enjoys the advantage of being able to creatively and flexibly deploy patrol resources in a manner which can significantly impact patterns of crime and disorder. This gives transit commanders both a greater opportunity and responsibility toward developing and implementing appropriate strategies. McDonald notes that urban police generally spend about 90 percent of their time in activities related to reacting or responding to calls for service, leaving approximately 10 percent of their duty time available for directed patrol. Noting that transit policing is primarily self-directed—with these percentages generally reversed—she makes a strong case for creative use of police presence to enhance rider confidence and deter criminal activity.

Since transit patrons move throughout a system removed from their familiar neighborhood environment with fixed police facilities and readily identifiable patrol resources, transit police must build perceptions of security and familiarity through heightened presence. The mere presence of uniformed patrol officers, however, will not suffice, since police who simply stand a post without being actively engaged in tangible activity are frequently viewed as a non-police presence, reinforcing negative assumptions that there is a lack of will or commitment to controlling the transportation system. McDonald observes that structured police activity—including frequent interaction with passengers, and the citing, warning or ejection of rules violators—is essential, pointing out that "police activity can be a striking means of impressing passengers that the police are present and energetically engaged in protecting them and controlling rules violators or potential criminals." She identifies this active role as a vital management priority, stating that "the role of the commander and supervisors in motivating police officers to engage in police activity is paramount . . . Officers must understand the importance of their work and its implications for crime control, and the public's perception of its own safety."

Fear of Crime

These issues are not limited to urban rail systems. They are equally important at airports, passenger ship terminals, seaports—all public transportation facilities. As Vincent Del Castillo, a former Chief of the New York City Transit Police Department and professor of law, police science and criminal justice at New York's John Jay College of Criminal Justice has observed, "passenger confidence and indeed public transportation usage are strongly related to the perception of safety in public transportation systems."[5] After reviewing fear of crime in terms of who is fearful, the police response to this fear, increased police visibility and aggressive enforcement tactics, Del Castillo concludes that transportation police need to develop routine, continuous fear-of-crime monitoring of transit passengers. Such monitoring would provide police managers and strategists with the tools necessary to evaluate the impact of patrol strategies in the light of passenger fear.

In developing his rationale for fear reduction efforts, Del Castillo reviews the results of a 1988 New York Metropolitan Transportation Authority survey examining fear of subway crime victimization. His study evaluating this survey[6] found that of 996 New York City residents responding, about 10 percent reported ever being a victim of a serious crime in the subway and 24 percent reported observing a serious subway crime occur. Yet over 70 percent of the respondents were worried about being the victim of a serious subway crime when riding the system after 8:00 P.M.

Characteristics related both to *individuals* and *environment* were assessed in order to determine the parameters associated with fear of subway crime. Briefly, individual characteristics associated with this fear were gender, age, race and prior personal knowledge of subway victimization. The study found that women, the elderly and Asians were most fearful of criminal victimization.

Environmental factors were found to be strong indicators of perceived social control, with "the appearance or perception of disorderly and uncivil behavior . . . considered signals of a breakdown of social control." Del Castillo observed that "incivilities and disorder in the subways were related to fear" and notes that "factors most closely related to that fear were graffiti and people being hassled by youths."

These observations summarize important concerns for the police who protect and secure transportation facilities used by the public anywhere in the world. When combined with an understanding of other security issues discussed in previous chapters—such as physical security measures for cargo handling facilities; the threats associated with theft, fraud or drug trafficking; the illegal movements of persons and goods; the threat of terrorism and piracy; the risks associated with moving hazardous and dangerous goods; and emergency management at all types of facilities—police executives and planners are able to develop meaningful responses to the issues associated with policing transportation facilities.

Specialized vs. General Service

Transportation facilities of all types are secured and policed by a variety of police agencies. In some cases these agencies are specialized and protect a specific facility or type of transportation system (i.e., a port authority police force, a transit police force, railway police, airport police). In other cases, general service police at a local, state, regional or national level protect the facility. These officers can be special dedicated units of a general agency, operating by mandate or via a contract (or purchase of service agreement) or their duties can be performed as part of their general duties without special consideration. In either case, police services at these facilities can be and often are supplemented by site-specific security forces (either proprietary or contracted).

In many cases, mixtures or hybrid arrangements are in place, with several police and security providers contributing to different facets of the effort to police, secure and protect any particular transit system or type of facility. With a number of law enforcement and security agencies contributing to an overall security and social control program, a high degree of coordination and cooperation must be maintained. While many models of service delivery for transportation facilities are possible, the need for integration, cooperation and coordination of services remain constant no matter which framework is adopted.

Separate agencies are often responsible for dealing with different segments of a comprehensive policing effort. While setting its own objectives and defining its own measures of success, each agency is an appendage of a disaggregated social control network. Insulation allows each agency to avoid uncertainty by negotiating its own institutional environment.

Three central tendencies can be observed in the organizational behavior of these agencies. First, organizations tend to splinter in order to insulate themselves and control their environments. Second, as organizations become more separate and parochial, they tend to restrict the access and flow of information with other parts of the same organization or with compatriot organizations. Also, coordination and cooperation with other organizations frequently becomes limited and difficult to achieve. Third, as organizations institutionalize their independence, they tend to duplicate the functions of similar organizations.

Consolidation of similar agencies has frequently been offered as a means to cope with these issues. Fiscal retrenchment has renewed examination of service delivery mechanisms in efforts to improve effectiveness and stabilize operational costs.

Police agencies in particular, due to increasing demand for services and diminishing fiscal support, need to evaluate methods to maximize service delivery and enhance cost effectiveness. Consolidation or merger of a number of small departments into "regional" agencies is frequently cited as an attractive organizational alternative.

Supporters of consolidation claim that merger eliminates (or reduces) duplication of effort, reduces equipment and logistical expenditures, and increases personnel effectiveness by allowing for more specialization and greater career mobility and promotional opportunity.

Opponents of consolidation feel that police service is best delivered on a more local, personal level. Some analysts support a middle ground where certain functions are centralized, but departments (and localities) maintain autonomy. Functions most commonly consolidated or regionalized are communications, training and automated information systems.

Which type of police service delivery model is most effective, particularly in the transportation environment? This question is difficult to answer, since no simple solution exists and the answer may vary from community to community, system to system, facility to facility. Clearly, the delivery of all police services—not just transportation services—is fragmented. In the worst case, this fragmentation has the potential to result in overlapping or duplicated services. Conversely, the fragmentation may allow for tailored, location-appropriate customized response. Either way, police protection as a whole cannot be adequate in any jurisdiction if it is not adequate in adjacent jurisdictions. Cooperation and coordination among agencies is necessary to combat criminal activity which transcends jurisdictional (and in a transportation setting, modal) boundaries.

Although consolidation of police agencies has been a popular theme in police management and studies for the past 25 to 30 years, much work still needs to be done and little consensus exists. Many statistical and econometric models are difficult to apply and require a degree of technical sophistication which intimidates some police administrators and political bodies. Further, existing analysis and research often presents conflicting results. Nevertheless, consolidation of general police agencies has had positive effects in Great Britain and in parts of the United States.

Regardless of economic or operational benefits, the political dimension of consolidation cannot be ignored. Localities, including the operators of transportation facilities, are reluctant to relinquish the power they possess, even with the prospect of greater economy or improved quality of services. This is particularly true when one considers that specialized transportation police agencies often arose as a result of lack of attention on the part of local police entities.

Research on consolidation is available to assist police and transportation facility administrators in selecting the appropriate model for policing their particular system or facility. E. Toporek and G.H. Burns, two researchers at Arizona State University, have argued in favor of consolidation, claiming that a lack of uniformity among localities and a multiplicity of jurisdictional levels inhibits the effectiveness of American policing. They argue that "lack of cooperation and even direct competition between agencies must be eliminated"[7] if the police service is to adequately meet its goals. Similarly, H.P. Pachnon and N.P. Lourich, Jr. in a 1977 survey of urban police services and consolidation[8] note that community and individual satisfaction with police services is not a function of municipal size but rather a reflection of the differentiated socioeconomic characteristics of central cities. They suggest that evidence shows that if socioeconomic and other factors are held equal and constant, larger jurisdictions will provide more satisfying police services. On the other hand, in *Policing in Metropolitan America,*[9] E. Ostrom, R.B. Parks and G.P. Whitaker examined municipal police agencies in small to medium-sized localities for instances of duplication, confusion and noncooperation. They found little evidence of any of these factors, leading the authors to determine that police reorganization needs to be based on realistic assessments of the needs of each individual area.

In his solo work, "On Righteousness, Evidence and Reform—The Police Story,"[10] E. Ostrom concludes that there is no evidence to support the contention that consolidation leads to improved or less costly police services. He maintains that smaller police agencies generally provide better quality field services at lower cost than larger ones. He also found some evidence that medium-sized agencies are the most effective and least costly to run. He argues that while some economies of scale may result from consolidating certain support services, there are indications that consolidated field services can reduce the quality of services delivered while increasing the cost of delivery.

Norman C. Walzer, an economist, notes in his 1970 doctoral dissertation "Economies of Scale and Municipal Police Services"[11] that when governments began to feel financial pressure due to increasing population and the fragmented nature of the local state, consolidation began to be considered as a method of alleviating fiscal constraints, since larger units of government may be able to provide services at a lower cost and may, in fact, be necessary for the provision of adequate levels of service. After considering a number of economic and structural factors, Walzer concludes (with the qualification that further research is needed) that it is possible that a larger governmental unit could provide better quality police services at a lower cost (i.e., as agencies become larger through consolidation, per unit cost of police activities decreases).

What does this mean for transportation policing? Some studies have argued that consolidation results in a lower cost for providing service of a higher quality. Others have demonstrated that consolidation will result in higher costs and lower service quality. The one area of agreement among researchers is that individual communities have different needs.

This may be particularly true when considering the structure for policing transportation facilities. The advantages of economics and efficiency have been used to argue *against* consolidation of specialized police agencies. For example, Thomas J. Sardino, past president of the International Association of Chiefs of Police (IACP), in his 1984 President's Message pointed out that specialized policing refers to law enforcement agencies which provide service to specific industries. Included in this definition are airport and seaport police; bridge, tunnel and turnpike police; mass transit police, and the like. Sardino termed specialized policing "regulatory policing" since the functions of their specialized agencies (industries) which the police protect are often regulated by various federal regulatory authorities (e.g., the Federal Aviation Administration). Sardino argues that these regulatory police agencies are indispensable, stating that "common to the need for specialized policing in these areas is a technical expertise in the industry being served. Since few full service police departments can afford the luxury of staffing their agencies with in-house experts on the diverse technology that permeates advanced societies, a regulatory law enforcement has emerged as a more effective and efficient means of control."[12]

Acknowledging the constraint on municipal spending that faces many police agencies, he notes that "involving our regulatory agencies with greater means of policing their industries will benefit general service agencies suffering from reduced spending and limited resources."

Sardino predicted that specialized police agencies would become increasingly important, stating in his President's Message that "regulatory policing provides an immeasurable service to public safety and security, and facilitates an orchestrated professional interaction within the law enforcement community. As greater urbanization continues to concentrate large numbers of people in the inner cities and their suburbs, there quickly follows the support services of mass transit systems . . . and the need for regulatory functions. While these movements bring additional work loads to the full-service police in terms of increased crime, regulatory law enforcement significantly relieves general service for their primary role of crime abatement."

This view reflects the traditional thinking in terms of specialized or regulatory theories but recent trends, especially in California where contract policing is common, find many local law enforcement agencies coming to view consolidated police service provision as desirable. Stimulated by the broader view of policing articulated in community and problem-oriented policing, these agencies consider the transportation infrastructure an integral part of the community as a whole and advocate coordinated and integrated policing at these facilities and systems within the broader general system of police service delivery. Rather than viewing specialized policing—such as transit policing—a detriment to their broader role, many general service agencies view it as a natural adjunct to these services, allowing for a comprehensive problem-solving and crime and order maintenance posture.

Under this view, necessary technical skills are developed by dedicated specialized subunits of the broader department, who benefit from common training and links with the larger agency. Responsiveness to the specialized environment of the transportation facility or system is ensured through contractual agreements which specify a predetermined level of coverage stipulated by the transportation facility, which purchases these services on a contract basis. This hybrid service delivery framework allows transportation facilities to benefit from a dedicated force committed to serving the facility's needs while allowing their police arm to enjoy the benefits of integration with the local police agency.

As previously discussed, the desirability of the consolidation of police services is unclear. Each individual community and each individual transportation facility or system must, by virtue of its own unique environment, priorities, usage and needs, find its own answers to this question. Regardless of the structure adopted to police a particular transit facility, alternative models for delivering police services should be thoroughly investigated and evaluated. To do so, meaningful measures of police productivity, inputs, outputs, service quality and cost efficiency need to be developed and analyzed. Without qualitative and quantitative analysis and research which accurately measure the relationship between these factors and the goals of the police service and the transportation provider, no model of service delivery can be recommended for a particular system.

No matter which model is selected, the issues and problems facing the police or security force which protects a transportation system will remain the same. Many of the issues, problems and threats to transit facilities discussed in this text will present themselves.

Regardless of agency type, we strongly suggest that the concepts of community policing and problem-solving be adopted, not as a program but rather as the underlying philosophy for developing a meaningful policing package for the transportation facility.

When considering how community policing and problem-solving can be adopted in total or in part to a transportation police environment, it is useful to have a common definition of the word "problem." Simply stated, a problem is a cluster of similar, related or recurring incidents that become a community or patron concern, thus forming a unit of police activity. According to Herman Goldstein in his book *Problem-oriented Policing,* [13] problems are typically characterized as being related to behavior, territory, persons and time.

In the transit setting, *behavior* may include panhandling, boisterous or unruly activity, alcohol or drug use, graffiti writing, trespassing and the like. *Territory* involves passenger stations, terminals, park-and-ride lots, specific right-of-ways, yards, shops, railcars on a specific line, docks, quays, stevedoring and cargo handling facilities, gangways, vessels, outports, channels, perimeters, runways, intermodal transport points and so on.

Defining a problem according to *persons* may entail groups of offenders (e.g., truants, panhandlers, pickpockets, stowaways), victims (e.g., the elderly or women) or complainants. Additionally, classes of people—such as transit personnel, commuters or shopkeepers—who use or sustain the system or facility may be classed within this dimension. Repeat offenders or groups (e.g., youth or street gangs) or common conditions distinguishing individuals such as mental illness, alcoholism or homelessness would fall into this grouping.

Finally, *time* is an important dimension for grouping problems. In the transit setting, important temporal events include peak hours, non-peak hours, school hours, non-revenue hours, and so on. Special events, weekends and holidays are also linked to this dimension. At seaports, temporal elements include embarkation or disembarkation; similarly, at airports peak passenger loading, unloading and baggage claim hours become critical.

It is important to recognize that a specific problem definition may include elements of more than one of these dimensions. Also, successful problem-solving requires that problems be classed in ways meaningful to the specifics of transport policing and its environment.

Problem-solving offers a strong methodology for addressing issues encountered by police at transportation facilities. Rather than being a static, rote approach, problem-solving is dynamic in nature, allowing police to develop realistic approaches to changing conditions. Police efforts are enhanced since input is encouraged from all facets of the transit environment: from the officers themselves, system and facility management, transit customers and employees, and the impacted surrounding communities.

Challenges Ahead

This is particularly valuable since the problems of crime, disorder and terrorist violence which face transportation facilities change over time. Criminals adjust their tactics as the police employ successful countermeasures.

The advent of containerized shipping, for example, while initially reducing pilferage as a major concern at seaports, was replaced by thefts of entire containers and the fraudulent manipulation of shipments. As container cargo handling facilities became more secure, the hijacking of motor trucks transporting containers began to occur more frequently. Similarly, as car alarms and antitheft devices become effective at countering vehicle burglaries and thefts, criminals have begun stealing occupied cars—the recent trend known as "carjacking." Terrorists, too, have shifted tactics over the years. As passenger screening has made aircraft hijacking more difficult, bombings and assaults of air terminals have increased as a preferred method of attack.

Changes in travel mode and political and economic factors also influence the issues faced by transportation police. Customs unions, such as the creation of a single European market pursuant to the Maastract treaty, will add new concerns for police at European air and seaports. Internal borders will be replaced with a broader continental frontier. Enhanced cooperation and intelligence sharing, as well as a need for greater understanding of police procedures at distant ports of entry, are likely results of these changes.

Developments in transportation technology will also alter the issues facing transport police. A renewed reliance on urban and commuter rail will stimulate the development of transit policing in cities which heretofore never had the need. High speed rail will spread the need for these special skills across state lines into new regions, and across international frontiers. The English Channel Tunnel (the "Chunnel") will provide a rail link between Britain and the European continent which will require British Transport Police and their French counterparts to explore new cooperative measures. Similar expansions in the role of transport policing can be expected throughout the world.

These challenges, combined with the increasing interdependence of nationstates throughout the world, will stimulate economic growth resulting in enhanced trade and movement of people. Due to these trends, transportation policing can be expected to take on an increasingly important role. *Policing Transportation Facilities* was prepared with this need in mind. It is our hope that this text will serve as a foundation for a better understanding and continued professional development of this important discipline.

Endnotes

1. See Eck and Spelman, *et al*, *Problem Solving: Problem-oriented Policing in Newport News* (Washington, D.C.: Police Executive Research Forum, 1987).

2. See George L. Kelling, "Police and their Communities: The Quiet Revolution" in National Institute of Justice *Perspectives on Policing* (Washington, D.C.: 1988). For an excellent review of this movement, see the series *Perspectives on Policing* by Howard University and the National Institute of Justice.

3. Kelling and Bratton, "Transit Police and Their Communities," *Transit Policing: A journal for the transit police service* (Vol. 1, No. 1, Fall 1991).

4. Phyllis McDonald, "Developing Patrol Tactics and Strategies for Transit Policing," *Transit Policing: A journal for the transit police service* (Vol. 2, No. 1, Summer/Fall 1992).

5. Vincent Del Castillo, "Fear of Crime: The Police Response," *Transit Policing: A journal for the transit police service* (Vol. 3, No. 1, Winter/Spring 1993).

6. Vincent Del Castillo, "Fear of Crime in the New York City Subway" (doctoral dissertation, Fordham University, New York, 1992).

7. E. Toporek and G.H. Burns, *Historical Perspectives of Police Development in America*, Arizona State University, NCJRS Microfiche Program (NCJ-27267).

8. H.P. Pachnon and N.P. Lourich, Jr., "Consolidation of Urban Police Services— A Focus on the Police," *Public Administration Review* (Vol. 37, No. 1, January/February 1977).

9. E. Ostrom, R.B. Parks and G.P. Whitaker, *Policing Metropolitan America* (Washington, D.C.: National Science Foundation).

10. E. Ostrom, *On Righteousness, Evidence and Reform—The Police Story* (NCJRS Microfiche Program, NCJ-29529).

11. N.C. Walzer, *Economies of Scale and Municipal Police Services* (doctoral dissertation, University of Illinois, University Microfilms, Ann Arbor, 1970).

12. Thomas J. Sardino, "Specialized Policing: The Contributions of Regulatory Law Enforcement" (IACP President's Message), *The Police Chief* (Vol. 11, No. 12, December 1984).

13. Herman Goldstein, *Problem-oriented Policing* (New York: McGraw-Hill, 1990).

APPENDIX

RAIL-DIRECTED TERRORISM

Introduction

Rail transit systems—both light and heavy rail—provide terrorists with highly visible targets. Because they are representative of government authority and carry large numbers of people in an unsecured environment, rail transit systems are susceptible to extensive disruption. Rail vehicles in transit systems also offer terrorists targets which are virtually impossible to secure.

Islamic extremists, Armenian nationalists, and Basque, Sikh and Tamil separatists are examples of terrorist groups which have threatened to or actually directed terrorist attacks against rail targets. Other groups which have relied on rail-directed terrorist acts include the Japanese leftist "Chukaku-Hu" ("Middle Core"), Peru's "Sendero Luminoso" ("Shining Path"), and Chile's "MIR" ("Movement of the Revolutionary Left"—Movimiento de Izquierda Revolucionaria) and "FTMR" (the "Manuel Rodriquez Terrorist Front"-Frente Terroristo Manuel Rodriquez). Nations which have experienced rail-directed terrorism include Japan, France, Spain, Switzerland, Israel, South Africa, the Netherlands, the United Kingdom, India, Sri Lanka, Chile, Italy, Iran, Burma and Canada.

"Sendero Luminoso" has frequently employed rail-directed terrorism in its insurgency in Peru. In 1984, for example, "Sendero Luminoso" exploited the economic impacts of rail-directed terrorism by blowing up a strategic railroad bridge east of Lima, effectively terminating vital food and mineral shipments ("Terrorists Knock Out Rail Bridge to Lima," Washington *Times,* 26 June 1984).

Throughout 1985 and 1986 Japanese terrorists carried out extensive assaults on Tokyo's subway system. In one notable attack in 1985, members of "Chukaku-Hu" attacked 34 nodes of the Japan National Railway system, shutting it down and stranding 18 million commuters by destroying electronic signaling devices (John Burgess, "High-tech Attacks Worry Japanese," Washington *Post,* 25 December 1985).

Statistical Information

Of 42 actual or attempted terrorist attacks directed against mass transit targets worldwide during the three year period December 1983–September 1986, there were 7 attempts or threats, 2 cases of civil disorder, and 33 actual terrorist assaults.

Of the 33 assaults, 2 cases involved sabotage and 31 cases were bombing incidents (including multiple bombings and arson). Additionally, there was one case of shooting subsequent to a bombing. Twenty-four attacks were directed against rail targets, 3 against buses, and 6 against terminals or stations. Rail-directed assault had an incidence four times greater than terminals or station-directed assault. Rail incidents occurred eight times more often than bus-targeted incidents.

The Chilean Experience

Chile experienced 78 rail-directed, explosive-related terrorist incidents in 1986. Twelve of these incidents occurred in metropolitan Santiago, while the remaining 66 occurred in outlying areas. Chilean police attribute these incidents to "MIR" and "FTMR." (*New Reflections on Terrorism and Terrorism in America — International Connections* by Fernando Paredes Pizarro, translated into English from *Nuevas Reflexiones Respecto al Terrorismo y El Terrorismo en America — Conexiones Internacionales,* Office of International Criminal Justice, University of Illinois, Chicago, 1987.)

Casualties—The Italian Experience

Bologna Railway Station Bombing—2 August 1980

291 injured
73 dead at scene
17 dead at hospital
118 admitted to hospital
9 admitted to ICU

Terrorist Attack on Train "Italicus"—4 August 1974

(40 km from Bologna)
48 injured
12 dead
23 admitted to hospital
4 admitted to ICU

Terrorist Attack on Train "904"—23 December 1986

(50 km from Bologna)
193 injured
12 dead
86 admitted to hospital
6 admitted to ICU
(Source: Bologna Soccorso)

The Threat of Extraordinary Violence—CBN Agents

The following excerpt from *Final Warning: Averting Disaster in the New Age of Terrorism* by Robert Kupperman and Jeff Kamen (New York: Doubleday, 1989, p.

106) succinctly describes the threat of chemical, biological or nuclear (CBN) agents against mass transit.

> In the late 1950s and early 1960s, government personnel conducted experiments to gauge the effects of biological attacks in the U.S. Using a non-lethal substitute for anthrax, they dropped light bulbs full of the powder in the subway system in New York City. The enormous winds created by the on-rushing trains distributed the powder through the tunnel system. Measurements taken indicated that hundreds of thousands of people would have died, had the attack been real.

Rail-directed Terrorism: Selected Incident Scenarios

24 September 1986, Tokyo, Japan

Signal cables and communication lines of the Japanese National Railways were vandalized, disrupting train service. Service delays inconvenienced approximately one million Tokyo commuters. Japanese police suspect left wing activists including "Chukaku-Hu" were responsible. "Chukaku-Hu" was responsible for similar acts in 1985.

26 June 1986, Cuzco, Peru

"Sendero Luminoso" explodes a time delayed device on a tourist train to Machu Picchu. Reports of this explosive attack vary. Impact has been reported as either 7 dead, 38 injured or 8 dead, 38 wounded (at least one dead and 17 wounded are believed to be U.S. citizens).

12 June 1986, New Delhi, India

Nine Sikh activists are arrested for conspiring with Canadian-based Sikhs to carry out a variety of terrorist acts, including the derailing of trains.

27 May 1986, Mediterranean Coast, Spain

"ETA" (Basque separatists) issues a communique threatening a terrorist campaign. A similar threat issued in 1985 preceded a series of bombings, including attacks on train stations.

7 May 1986, Tokyo, Japan

Early morning explosions rocked nearly 20 subway stations, marking the conclusion of the Tokyo Economic Summit. No injuries resulted.

6 May 1986, Tokyo, Japan

Morning rush hour subway service was disrupted by a series of small explosions, stranding millions of commuters.

30 March 1986, Lima, Peru

Leftist guerrillas bomb three points on Peru's central railroad, severing links between Lima and the Andes and wounding one person.

20 March 1986, Paris, France

Attempted bombing on crowded commuter train by Islamic extremists seeking release of comrades in French jails averted when police defuse bomb. "Committee of Solidarity with Arab and Middle Eastern Prisoners" claims responsibility.

20 December 1985, Santiago, Chile

Armed terrorists hold up a train at a Santiago railway station, then carry out a bombing of the station. Two policemen are shot during the escape.

29 November 1985, Tokyo, Japan

"Chakaku-Hu" carries out a series of coordinated attacks against rail targets across Japan. Signal equipment was sabotaged in 34 places, with 23 attacks occurring in metropolitan Tokyo. Additionally, the Asakusabashi Station in eastern Tokyo was set ablaze by 20–30 radicals. Forty-eight leftist rebels were arrested.

22 November 1985, Chandigarh, India

Two passengers are killed and 18 wounded when Sikh terrorists explode a bomb on a crowded train.

23 October 1985, Santiago, Chile

Fourteen bombs are detonated along railway lines linking Chile's major cities.

21 September 1985, New York City, U.S.

Thirty passengers injured when a gang of youths toss a smoke bomb into an IRT #4 (Lexington Avenue Express) train between 138th Street and the Grand Concourse in the South Bronx.

20 August 1985, Sri Lanka

Rebel guerrillas detonate a bomb outside the Vavoniya Train Station, killing 5 police officers. Eight additional persons were killed when the rebels subsequently swept the area with automatic weapons fire. The rebels then hijacked a train with 500 passengers aboard. The hijacking lasted five hours until the engineer deliberately derailed the train. The rebels fled with 15 hostages, who remain missing. According to unconfirmed reports, these passengers were later shot.

3 June 1985, Geneva, Switzerland

A bomb exploded in the main train station causing damage but no injuries.

11 May 1985, New Delhi, India

Sikh extremists explode bombs hidden in transistor radios on trains and buses without warning. Eighty killed, 150 injured.

19 April 1985, Colombo, Sri Lanka

High explosives detonated at the train station serving Colombo International Airport on the eve of a visit by British Prime Minister Margaret Thatcher. One killed, 3 injured.

3 April 1985, Toronto, Canada

Armenian terrorists threaten to bomb the subway system.

19 January 1985, Amsterdam, the Netherlands

Supporters of the "Red Army Faction" halt an interurban express train by pulling the emergency brake. The train was then spray painted with pro-RAF slogans.

23 December 1984, Rome, Italy

Militant neo-fascists detonate a bomb on a train inside a tunnel, killing 24 and injuring 186.

7 December 1984, Santiago, Chile

Terrorists bomb railway station during rush hour.

3 December 1984, Belfast, Ulster

"IRA" guerrillas derail train with explosives packed in beer kegs.

3 September 1984, Montreal, Canada

A bomb protesting the arrival of Pope John Paul II explodes inside a locker in Montreal's main railway station, killing 3 and wounding 59.

30 August 1984, Tehran, Iran

Twenty people are killed and 300 wounded when a bomb explodes in Tehran's main railway station.

17 August 1984, Grenoble, France

The Grenoble train station is bombed by a group claiming to have detonated two similar devices during the same week. The group demanded $3.75 million to stop their attacks.

30 April 1984, Santiago, Chile

The city's subway service is disrupted when a bomb explodes, injuring 20.

26 April 1984, New Delhi, India

Morning rush hour rail traffic is disrupted by three bombings.

15 April 1984, Amritsar, India

Thirty-one train stations are set afire, 4 others are bombed, and signal and communications facilities are sabotaged on the railways in the Punjab, by Sikh terrorists.

27 March 1984, Jerusalem, Israel

Explosive experts dismantle two bombs outside Jerusalem's train station.

2 March 1984, Santiago, Chile

Rail lines throughout Chile experience bombings resulting in at least 8 injuries.

19 January 1984, Rangoon, Burma

Ten people injured when train outside Rangoon is bombed.

20 January 1984, Hendaye, France

Fifteen pounds of explosives were found at the railway station at the Spanish border.

31 December 1983, Marseille, France

Two time-delayed explosive devices were exploded by terrorists, killing 4 and injuring 39. One device was left in the Marseille train station and the other was located aboard a high-speed train.

INDEX

155